Michelle McClain is an experience body of Christ. In this book you will gain practical instruction as well as insight into the mysteries of the prophetic flow. I have had the privilege of serving with Michelle at conferences and local church meetings on many occasions. I have also been in several planning meetings with her. I know Michelle to be a woman of integrity. I also know her to be transparent about her life and ministry preparation. This honest openness is a powerful tool for encouraging and equipping the people of God to utilize the prophetic anointing in their personal and ministry development. While reading this book you will experience this tool as you are equipped to prophesy with accuracy and clarity.

—Greg Howse
Senior Leader, Cornerstone Christian Center
Founder and President, Sharpening Stone
Ministries International
www.sharpeningstoneministries.com

I have found Michelle McClain to be a true New Testament prophet with a unique grace to teach, train, and activate believers to move in prophetic ministry. She knows how to come beside a senior leader with both sensitivity and true kingdom authority to help equip the saints and build the local church. Our people who have participated in her workshops always come away with fresh understanding of the office of the prophet and the biblical role of prophetic ministry in the church today. The belief "I can do that" fills the atmosphere when she teaches and trains. This book is a great resource for those who are looking to move in the prophetic as well as those who are seasoned.

—Michael Posey
Church of the Harvest
Evansville, IN

This book is a must read for all who would function in prophetic ministry and those who desire to deepen their understanding of how God releases His voice. Michelle McClain's experience and practical insights concerning the ministry of the prophet will propel the reader into new dimensions of prophetic ministry.

—BILL AND VENNER ALSTON
APOSTOLIC LEADERS OF CITY CHURCH
MILWAUKEE, WI

I recommend this book to any church or prophets desiring to enter fully into the next move of God. Michelle's prophetic insights in this book shed light on the church that is yet to emerge. Michelle will challenge you to rise up in strength and sharpen your prophetic edge. This book is like having a private tutor helping you to discover God's purpose for your prophetic life.

I was with Michelle recently in South Africa, and I witnessed the seven spirits of God manifest through her teaching. I saw men and women weeping because of the release of the prophetic word of God through Michelle. Michelle has been instrumental in birthing a greater release of the prophetic here at World Harvest Ministries

This is a resource guide that is much needed to help further launch those who are already established and transitioning into the prophetic.

—ALVIN AND ALVA GREEN
APOSTLES OF WORLD HARVEST MINISTRIES
COLUMBIA, SC

Michelle McClain is a prophet who embodies the essence of her office and calling. Her passion and wealth of wisdom to empower an emerging generation of prophetic believers are evident from the introduction. I believe this book will serve as a catalyst to launch many into their destiny, especially those who have longed for something fresh yet relevant on the prophetic. The cutting-edge insight on the seven spirits of God along with the plethora of experience she has shared in this book is truly inspiring. Read and reap the advantage.

—Stephen A. Garner
Rivers of Living Water Ministries International
Chicago, IL

Prophetess Michelle McClain is a profound teacher in the prophetic ministry and has a keen discerning gift that is manifested prophetically through words of wisdom and words of knowledge. We have had the opportunity and benefit of experiencing her time-tested, authentic prophetic ministry on numerous occasions, specifically at the church that we oversee (Divine Grace Ministries). McClain has the ability to flow in the anointing with both accuracy and integrity; such a combination helps to expand and elevate the expectations of God's people. As you dig into the book, you will find that her prophetic mantle allows her to exemplify how to walk in demonstrated spiritual power in a most excellent way. Prophetess McClain has a gift of exhortation that is a valuable asset for the praise and worship ministry in the assembly, and she is also able to minister with humility and meekness, bringing about positive kingdom-impacting results.

We highly recommend her as a minister of profound spiritual insight, consistency, and wisdom. She has a desire to edify the people of God through the spiritual gifts of the Holy Spirit.

The information in this book will be a valuable addition to your library and an excellent reference resource for your continual spiritual growth.

—Apostle Bobby and Prophetess Mary Johnson
Senior Pastors, Divine Grace Ministries
Burton, MI

THE
PROPHETIC
ADVANTAGE

Michelle McClain

CHARISMA
HOUSE

Most CHARISMA HOUSE BOOK GROUP products are available at special quantity discounts for bulk purchase for sales promotions, premiums, fund-raising, and educational needs. For details, write Charisma House Book Group, 600 Rinehart Road, Lake Mary, Florida 32746, or telephone (407) 333-0600.

THE PROPHETIC ADVANTAGE by Michelle McClain
Published by Charisma House
Charisma Media/Charisma House Book Group
600 Rinehart Road
Lake Mary, Florida 32746
www.charismahouse.com

Unless otherwise noted, all Scripture quotations are from the King James Version of the Bible.

Scripture quotations marked AMP are from the Amplified Bible. Old Testament copyright © 1965, 1987 by the Zondervan Corporation. The Amplified New Testament copyright © 1954, 1958, 1987 by the Lockman Foundation. Used by permission.

Scripture quotations marked GW are taken from God's Word, copyright © 1995 God's Word to the Nations. Used by permission of Baker Publishing Group.

Scripture quotations marked NAS are from the New American Standard Bible, copyright © 1960, 1962, 1963, 1968, 1971, 1972, 1973, 1975, 1977, 1995 by The Lockman Foundation. Used by permission. (www .Lockman.org)

Scripture quotations marked NET are from the NET Bible, copyright © 1996-2006 by Biblical Studies Press, L.L.C., http://bible.org. All rights reserved.

Scripture quotations marked NIV are from the Holy Bible, New International Version. Copyright © 1973, 1978, 1984, International Bible Society. Used by permission.

Scripture quotations marked NKJV are from the New King James Version of the Bible. Copyright © 1979, 1980, 1982 by Thomas Nelson, Inc., publishers. Used by permission.

Scripture quotations marked RSV are from the Revised Standard Version of the Bible. Copyright © 1946, 1952, 1971 by the Division of Christian Education of the National Council of the Churches of Christ in the USA. Used by permission.

Cover design by Justin Evans
Design Director: Bill Johnson

Visit the author's website at www.michellemcclainministries.com.

Library of Congress Cataloging-in-Publication Data:
An application to register this book for cataloging has been submitted to the Library of Congress.
International Standard Book Number: 978-1-61638-623-8
E-book ISBN: 978-1-62136-039-1

While the author has made every effort to provide accurate telephone numbers and Internet addresses at the time of publication, neither the publisher nor the author assumes any responsibility for errors or for changes that occur after publication.

First edition

12 13 14 15 16 — 9 8 7 6 5 4 3 2 1
Printed in the United States of America

As arrows are in the hand of a mighty man; so are children of the youth. Happy is the man that hath his quiver full of them: they shall not be ashamed, but they shall speak with the enemies in the gate.
[PSALM 127:4—5]

To Eboni, my beautiful, bold apostolic missionary, your passion for Jesus and desire to follow His prophetic purpose for your life at all cost are inspiring and challenging. Being your mother is the greatest joy of my life. I love you so much. Keep breaking limitations and equipping your generation with the prophetic advantage.

To all of my spiritual sons and daughters, it is has been an honor and privilege to mentor, train, and equip you to fulfill the God-given destiny over your lives. I am humbled that the Lord would allow me to influence so many of His great leaders of tomorrow. Knowing each one of you has made my life richer. You will be a part of the generation that will turn the world upside down.

Contents

Acknowledgments

WOULD LIKE TO take this opportunity to express my heartfelt gratitude to the following persons who have made the completion of this book possible.

To **Apostle John** and **Prophetess Wanda Eckhardt**, thank you for all of your wisdom and input into the project. As my spiritual parents you've always made room for me to accomplish great things in the earth. You've always challenged me to break limitations and barriers. Thank you for pushing me and at times rolling up your sleeves to help me complete this project. For this I am eternally grateful.

To **Sandra Norris**, my mentor, mother, and friend, thank you for all of your prayers, wisdom, love, and support. It is my desire that this book be a tribute and testament to your sacrifice and impartations made to my life.

To my sisters, **Latanza Woods** and **Rachel McClain**, thank you for all of your words of encouragement. Special thanks to Rachel for taking care of the natural things of my life while I spent countless hours at the computer writing.

To my auntie-mama **Nomia G. McClain**, thank you for exposing me to the finer things in life. Your sacrifice to make room for me in your life when I had nowhere else to live was pivotal in my life. I'm in this moment in time because of that moment in time.

I would also like to extend a special thank-you to the editorial team at Charisma House.

To **Jevon Bolden**, thank you for your patient guidance, enthusiastic encouragement, and useful critiques of this project. Your willingness to give your time so generously will forever be appreciated.

To **Barbara Dycus,** thank you for the initial valuable and constructive suggestions to the book.

To **Tessie Güell DeVore,** thank you for hearing and obeying the voice of the Lord. Your actions are a testament to the advantage the prophetic anointing provides.

Foreword

I AM HAPPY TO write the foreword for this new book on the prophetic ministry. I have seen the benefits and blessing of prophecy in my own life and in the life of the local church I am honored to lead. Michelle McClain has been a part of the development and growth of the prophetic ministry in Crusaders Church of Chicago.

The vision of our church has always been to activate and train people to operate in their God-given gifts. We have seen thousands of believers released to prophesy. We have spent countless hours teaching on the subject of prophecy and assisting emerging prophets in their training and development. Michelle has been instrumental in helping thousands of believers operate in a greater prophetic flow.

Michelle lives what she teaches and shares in this book. Her life is prophetic. This is why I highly recommend this book to all. I believe in impartation. I believe you will receive impartation as you read this book. Michelle has traveled around the world teaching on the prophetic ministry and activating believers and churches in prophecy. She is also a prophetic intercessor who has prayed for many to receive supernatural breakthroughs.

Prophecy gives believers an advantage. This book will give you a revelation of the benefits and blessing of prophecy. This can be seen in the life of Michelle McClain. I have personally witnessed her growth in the prophetic over the years. The result has been her life changing as well as being able to bless many worldwide.

The message in this book will challenge you to grow and expand in the prophetic ministry. There is always room for growth and expansion. We should never remain on the same level but continually grow in faith, giving us the ability to speak deeper and stronger. There are prophetic utterances that must be released over individuals, churches, and nations that will birth and accelerate the purposes of God. This is true for this generation and generations to come. We should abound in utterance.

Michelle's desire is to see the church rise up with a bold, reforming spirit to meet the challenges of this generation. The lion is the symbol of boldness. Boldness is necessary to function in the prophetic ministry. Prophets can no longer hide and cower in fear, but they must come forth and release the word of the Lord.

Michelle also has a desire to see the church arise in power through holiness and purity. Prophets must be pure, and they must release a pure word. Prophets call churches to holiness and help them do what is pleasing to God. This will come through in the pages of this book.

There is an increased interest in the prophetic ministry today. This interest is being birthed through the Holy Spirit. There is a need for sound, biblical teaching on this subject. We need books written that will combat the errors that come with any restoration movement. These books need to be written by people experienced in the subject and not by novices. Michelle's experience over many years will assist any new minister desiring to move in the prophetic.

I encourage those who lead prophetic ministries in their local churches to use this book to teach, train, and inspire emerging prophets and prophetic people. I am convinced this book will become a resource for many emerging ministers. This book will encourage you to fulfill your calling and obey God's prophetic directives. Let the church arise and speak to this generation.

—APOSTLE JOHN ECKHARDT
CRUSADERS CHURCH
AUTHOR OF *PRAYERS THAT ROUT DEMONS*

Y OU'RE NOT IN this world by chance. You're not in this decade by chance. I brought you into the place you are in now to teach and train. Yes," says the Spirit of God, "you are My handiwork, created for My good works. You've been called into ministry. I'll set it up. You will turn the corner, and you'll be right there in the middle of your destiny. I'm equipping you with a prophetic advantage."

"Advantage?" I thought to myself. "Well, it's about time, because I've been at nothing but a disadvantage all of my life." I knew the words I was hearing during this time of ministry were different. Actually I felt as if someone had just removed the death grip from around my neck that life had on me. The words that were coming out this man's mouth—each phrase, each syllable—began to remove the veil that trauma, tragedy, father rejection, and abandonment had placed upon my heart. These words were not normal words. These words were the prophetic words inspired by a true and living God who cared for me. These words were touching the very core of my existence. Up until this time I had received many awards and attended self-help seminars looking for some reason for my existence. Nothing began to answer the search for significance as these prophets did as they were proclaiming the plans and purposes of the Lord over my life.

This prophetic word thrust me from feeling meaningless to significant. It began to set my life on the course the Lord ordained for me. I never knew a woman could be called to preach. I was raised in a Baptist church that said women could not preach, so my being call into ministry was a concept I never dreamed of. I had to be renewed in the spirit of my mind before I could wrap my faith around this assignment.

The word that these prophets spoke over me awakened a passion in me to seek the Lord. I never knew God was personal and that I could have a relationship with Him. I never knew there were specific plans, purposes, gifts, and talents given to each person by God. The prophetic anointing added value, worth, and definition to my existence.

As I listened, I instantly knew that this was the voice that had been leading all of my life. This prophetic encounter sent me into a desperate search for answers to some serious questions I had for God. True prophetic ministry will always lead you to the feet of Jesus and not the feet of man. I actually felt peace and anger at the same time. I questioned, "If God's plans are so good for me, why has so much devastation happened in my life?"

My very first memory of encountering the prophetic surrounded the tragedy of watching my mother die from a rare blood disease. My mother was suffering with pain, and she kept complaining about people tormenting her. I remember seeing these "people," who I know now were demon spirits. I heard a voice say, "Michelle, say 'Jesus.'" I screamed, "Jesus!" And I saw those little troll-like men leave out of the window.

I've had this kind of leading all of my life. I remember when I was about seven years old there was a man who would always hang around the family. I never trusted this man. Something told me to watch him. My grandmother raised me, and she would have card parties. One particular night something told me to gather my two sisters and go into the back room to play. I really believe I was empowered by the spirit of counsel and might, because I pushed a five-drawer dresser in front of the door for protection. I remember this man stumbling to push on that door, but he couldn't get in. He later alarmed the adults about the dresser being in front of the door. My question has always been, "Why was he back there anyway?" This scenario could have ended quite differently if I hadn't responded to this voice.

I have been favored with these supernatural experiences at very critical times in my life—and all before I really knew the Lord or had any understanding about the prophetic. There was another God leading that happened in high school.

I was underage and attending a college party. Something told me to pay attention to the ratio of girls to boys at the party. As I looked around the room, as this voice instructed me to do, I realized that there were many more boys than girls. Right then I told my date that I needed to be excused to freshen up in the ladies' room. As I was on my way to the back door, I saw another classmate. I asked her to come with me to the restroom, so I wouldn't alarm her date. I knew she had a car, so I told her to grab her purse and follow me. We left that party through the back door. We heard the next day that many girls were gang-raped that night.

I know it was God's mercy that led me out of that place. It was His light piercing through the darkness of my heart to lead me to a place of safety. The young lady who was with me that night became my best friend, and we've been friends for more than thirty years.

Maybe you've not had these kinds of experiences, but we have all experienced that proverbial "something told me to…" We'll say, "Something told me not to go down that street," and later we find out that the worse accident in the history of highway existence occurred. That "something," that unknown voice that leads us out of trouble and into a place of goodness, is the voice of the Lord.

God has thoughts and plans to prosper each one of us. It was never His will for mankind to grope around in darkness not knowing what to do with the precious gift of life. He wants to lead us into paths of righteousness by sending us the gift of prophets who empower His people with a prophetic anointing. Jeremiah 29:11–13 states, "For I know the thoughts that I think toward you, says the LORD, thoughts of peace and not of evil, to give you a future and a hope. Then you will call upon Me and go and pray to Me, and I will listen to you. And you will seek Me and find Me, when you search for Me with all your heart" (NKJV).

What Is Prophecy?

Some people, based on their background, can get nervous when the conversation shifts to the prophetic. Some people think prophecy is emotionalism and something done only in charismatic or Pentecostal circles. Prophecy can really be seen from the wrong perspective, man's perspective. Prophecy is simply the revealed truth of who God is and His will for mankind. Prophecy can be further defined as speaking forth by divine inspiration the heart and mind of God to a particular people or certain situation. It is the dropping down of inspired speech into the hearts of men. Being God's creation, we need to know His heart for us. This is a valuable and vital element to our living well on the earth. We need to know God's heart and mind toward us.

The nature of prophecy has two dimensions: forth-telling and foretelling.

1. Forth-telling prophecy: This form of prophecy is in the realm of speaking forth—the prophet or believers speaking for God to the people, communicating the mind of God for the present.

2. Foretelling prophecy: This aspect of prophecy is in the form of prediction. The prophet speaks for God to the people, communicating His mind for the future. This level announces a new agenda on God's timetable for human history.

The authority and power of God are released through prophecy. Individuals, churches, and nations need to hear the word of the Lord. This is the key to the power and authority of the prophets:

they are spokesmen of God. Prophets carry the voice of the Lord to kings and nations. They speak as oracles of God.

God's voice commands the armies in heaven and in earth. He is the Lord of armies. The army of God hears His voice and carries out His word. The word of the Lord mobilizes His people. The voice of the Lord will mobilize the church.

> For he is our God; and we are the people of his pasture, and the sheep of his hand. To day if ye will hear his voice.
>
> —PSALM 95:7

We are the Lord's sheep, and we hear His voice. He leads us and guides us by His voice. This could be a still small voice, or it can be the word of prophecy. We need to hear His voice today, and we do this through the prophetic gifting ministered to us by prophets or prophetic believers or an impartation from the Lord Himself.

We need to be tuned in to what the Lord is speaking today. We need to know what He is saying to us in the present season. Prophets and prophetic people have their ears tuned to hear what the Lord is saying to His church today.

Prophecy will encourage you to move into the will of God. It releases faith to operate beyond what you are accustomed to. Prophecy breaks through demonic strongholds that are set up in the mind to hinder the plans and purposes for your life. The prophetic ministry, when delivered with accuracy and integrity, can restore the dignity and honor man lost in the garden.

About This Book

The Prophetic Advantage is a book about the strength and power of the prophetic ministry. This book will challenge you to rise up in strength, sharpen your prophetic edge, and release what God has given you, bringing change to your generation. It is designed to teach you how to discern the voice of God and respond appropriately using the revealed truth for your advantage in fulfilling your destiny. Being able to hear and discern the voice of the Lord is a process that comes in time.

God graciously makes Himself known to humanity since people cannot discover Him on their own. He achieves this in many ways but supremely through His Son, Jesus Christ. He also accomplishes this through His prophets and prophetic people.

A supernatural God can be known only supernaturally, by a supernatural revelation of Himself to the heart.

> God, who commanded the light to shine out of darkness, hath shined in our hearts, to give the light of the knowledge of the glory of God in the face of Jesus Christ.
>
> —2 CORINTHIANS 4:6

The Prophetic Advantage is not just a clever title created by my publishers. It was a prophetic promise revealed to me by the prophets during a time of prophetic ministry. I believe that just as God used prophets of old, the Lord uses the life of modern-day prophets as a model to His people. My life is a testimony of the advantage the prophetic gives to God's people when interpreted and applied correctly. It is a description of my life. I am a product of the prophetic ministry. To be prophetic means to hear the voice of God and respond. God's thoughts for me were so much higher than thoughts I thought of myself.

The Lord wants His creation to know His thoughts. Just because His thoughts are higher doesn't mean that they are not knowable. The Lord promised that He would tell us things to come. He will not leave us as orphans to grope for some sense of existence. Psalm 139 tells us there is a book with all of our days written in it before we ever live one out. God knows and desires to reveal our lives. He is not far away. He has a plan, but we must submit to His voice and obey.

Obeying and submitting to God's prophetic process has taken me around the world. I am just a little girl from the ghetto of Chicago raised on welfare, and I've preached in forty-six different countries. If God made that happen for me, He can make it happen for you.

> Your eyes saw my unformed substance, and in Your book all the days [of my life] were written before ever they took shape, when as yet there was none of them. How precious and weighty also are Your thoughts to me, O God! How vast is the sum of them! If I could count them, they would be more in number than the sand. When I awoke, [could I count to the end] I would still be with You.
> —PSALM 139:16–18, AMP

This passage of Scripture tells me that we are not in this world by accident. It doesn't matter how you got here. It may have been by a one-night stand or some other unplanned way. I believe you are reading this book because you are a child of destiny, and the Lord wants you to learn how to read your book of destiny written by an eternal God. He is the author of your life.

This book that you're holding is a product of prophecy. On October 18, 1996, Dr. Elsie Clark gave me a prophetic word that stated I would write books. On October 18, 1998, I received that same word from Dr. Sharon Stone. My publisher scheduled the release of this book, my first, for October 16, 2012. Prophecy is real, and if obeyed it will produce great blessings in your life.

Chapter 1

Releasing the Lion's Roar

And he said, The LORD will roar from Zion,
and utter his voice from Jerusalem.

—AMOS 1:2

After it a voice roareth: he thundereth with the voice of his
excellency; and he will not stay them when his voice is heard.

—JOB 37:4

THERE IS A roar coming out of the church in proclamations, decrees, praise, worship, and intercession that will prepare the way for the greatest awakening the world has ever seen. God will use His prophets to make way for this great awakening.

Prophets roar against injustice.

Prophets roar against sin and rebellion.

Prophets roar against idolatry.

Prophets roar against the enemies of God.

Prophets shine a light on the path of righteousness that will lead the way for the body of Christ to fulfill her destiny in God.

The Lionlike Nature of God

Jesus went to the cross as a lamb, but He arose as the Lion of the tribe of Judah prevailing over all the powers of darkness. The lionlike nature of the Lord is being expressed through His prophets and prophetic people. There is coming a reformation to the entire prophetic office and prophetic realm.

The word *reformation* comes from the Greek word *diorthosis*, and it means "making straight."[1] In a physical sense it refers to restoring to its natural and normal condition something that in some way protrudes or has gotten out of line, such as a broken or misshapen limb. It is where we get our English word *orthopedic*, which is the study of human skeletal structure. This word is associated with skeletal adjustments. It points to a change in the internal hidden skeleton that gives shape to the body.

The Lord is adjusting mentalities and heart positions to reflect the image and nature of Jesus Christ the prophet.

> The lion hath roared, who will not fear? the Lord GOD hath spoken, who can but prophesy?
> —AMOS 3:8

Amos declared the word of the Lord to Israel in a time of widespread rebellion and apostasy. He was the voice that represented the Lion's roar. His words were ones of dire warning. The people hearing them should have feared greatly.

Amos could not refrain from speaking. Prophetic people cannot refrain from declaring what the Lord is saying. When there is a stirring in the land, prophetic people cannot be silent.

The Lion of Judah lives inside of you. It is the nature of the lion to roar. The lion's roar is known to cause great fear in the animal kingdom. The lion's strength and power are manifested through his roar.

When God's people speak what God gives them with boldness, it is like a lion's roar. The roar of the lion will produce the fear of the Lord. This is one of the functions of true prophets: to release and help maintain the fear of the Lord in His church.

Prophetic voices are roaring against injustice. Prophetic voices are roaring against the powers of darkness. Prophetic voices are roaring against the enemies of the kingdom.

We are not zoo lions caged by religion and tradition, losing our ability to speak truth, muzzled by laws and tradition of men. We are not circus lions performing and entertaining prophetic words that tickle the ear and appease the flesh of men. The roar of the Lion of Judah is coming through His prophetic people even now.

The Attributes of the Lion

We are made in God's image and likeness. If we are to be holy as He is holy, we should also take on His lionlike character. Jesus showed us what this lionlike character would look like as it is lived out in everyday life. Through the power of the Holy Spirit we are to emulate the character of Christ. Jesus is the Lion of Judah, and He did only what He saw His Father do. Jesus did great works in the earth, but He said that we would do even greater works. What I want you to understand is that as I describe the attributes of the lion, I am speaking about you—the righteous ones. The righteous are as bold as lions. These are the attributes of the lion that God wants to impart to you.

Strength

> A lion which is strongest among beasts, and turneth not away
> for any.
> —PROVERBS 30:30

The lion is the strongest among beasts. We must be strong in the Lord and in the power of His might.

Valiance

> And he also that is valiant, whose heart is as the heart of a
> lion, shall utterly melt: for all Israel knoweth that thy father is
> a mighty man, and they which be with him are valiant men.
>
> —2 SAMUEL 17:10

Valiant means to possess valor, be brave, to be marked by or
done with valor. Valor is courage in the face of danger, especially
in battle. There must be courage in declaring the word of the Lord.
The Lord encouraged Joshua to be courageous (Josh. 1:6, 9). Many
believers are struggling with fear, and this is hindering them from
flowing in a high level of prophecy. We must be courageous in
confronting the powers of darkness with the word of the Lord.
There are too many who dilute the message, and many hide under
the cover of political correctness.

Fearlessness

> Where is the dwelling of the lions, and the feedingplace of the
> young lions, where the lion, even the old lion, walked, and the
> lion's whelp, and none made them afraid?
>
> —NAHUM 2:11

Prophetic people must not be afraid to confront and deal with
the strongholds in our society.

Boldness

> The wicked flee when no man pursueth: but the righteous are
> bold as a lion.
>
> —PROVERBS 28:1

Boldness is related to speech. (See Acts 19:8.) Those who are bold
will speak boldly. Fear will cause some to shut their mouths when

they should be speaking. Prophetic people who speak boldly will shatter the powers of darkness with their prophetic declarations. The Greek word for "boldness" is *parrēsia*, meaning freedom in speaking, unreservedness in speech, openly, frankly, that is, without concealment, without ambiguity or circumlocution, free and fearless confidence, cheerful courage, boldness, and assurance.[2]

One spoken word from lionlike believers under a prophetic mantle crushes every opposing force. "How forcible are right words!" says Job 6:25. This is divine enablement that comes upon ordinary people exhibiting power and authority.

The lion is known for boldness, fearlessness, power, valiance, and strength. Prophets and prophetic people must rise in boldness, courage, and strength to declare the word of the Lord in this age.

Lions must roar. A lion without a roar is not much of a lion. There is no place for fear and intimidation. We must confront Jezebel and the demons that seek to intimidate prophetic people. We need righteous prophets. We need prophets who declare righteousness. Righteousness produces boldness. The righteous need not fear, for God is on their side. God supports and defends the righteous.

Chapter 2

The Prophetic Advantage

*What advantage then hath the Jew? or what profit is
there of circumcision? Much every way: chiefly, because
that unto them were committed the oracles of God.*

—ROMANS 3:1–2

WE ARE LIVING in days of tremendous crisis and turmoil. The Lord has set the stage where no one with a carnal mind can discern what is happening in our society socially, economically, or militarily. If there was ever a time when God's people needed an advantage, it is now. The Lord in His mercy is releasing revelation knowledge through His prophets that will empower the people of God with wisdom, direction, and insight into the council of His will.

Israel had an advantage over the other nations because they possessed the oracles of God. "Oracle" is the Greek word *logion*, meaning "a brief utterance," "a divine oracle," and in the New Testament, "the words or utterances of God," "of the contents of the Mosaic law."[1] The prophetic Scriptures gave Israel an advantage in preparing them for the coming Messiah.

If any man speak, let him speak as the oracles of God; if any man minister, let him do it as of the ability which God giveth:

that God in all things may be glorified through Jesus Christ, to whom be praise and dominion for ever and ever. Amen.

—1 PETER 4:11

The Lord is empowering the church with an anointing to communicate His heart and mind accurately. The church will speak as an oracle of God. When we speak prophetically, we are speaking as the oracles of God. This will give us an advantage in all things pertaining to our lives. We have an advantage, just as Israel had an advantage. This is called the prophetic advantage.

Advantage means a condition or circumstance that puts one in a favorable or superior position. Prophecy gives us many advantages. We can prosper through prophecy.

God desires for His people to prosper. The Scriptures give us numerous references that connect prosperity to the prophetic ministry. Obeying God's voice was always a key to prosperity.

Consider these scriptures:

> And it shall come to pass, if thou shalt hearken diligently unto the voice of the LORD thy God, to observe and to do all his commandments which I command thee this day, that the LORD thy God will set thee on high above all nations of the earth: And all these blessings shall come on thee, and overtake thee, if thou shalt hearken unto the voice of the LORD thy God. Blessed shalt thou be in the city, and blessed shalt thou be in the field.
>
> —DEUTERONOMY 28:1–3

The key to prosperity and blessing is to obey the voice of the Lord. This is what makes us a peculiar treasure.

> Now therefore, if ye will obey my voice indeed, and keep my covenant, then ye shall be a peculiar treasure unto me above all people: for all the earth is mine.
>
> —EXODUS 19:5

God promises if we are willing and obedient, we will eat the good of the land. By obeying His voice, we will find that the land will provide us with blessing.

> If ye be willing and obedient, ye shall eat the good of the land.
>
> —ISAIAH 1:19

Notice how the people of God prospered through the prophesying of Haggai and Zechariah. They prospered in spite of much opposition to rebuilding the temple. This is the prophetic advantage.

> And the elders of the Jews builded, and they prospered through the prophesying of Haggai the prophet and Zechariah the son of Iddo. And they builded, and finished it, according to the commandment of the God of Israel, and according to the commandment of Cyrus, and Darius, and Artaxerxes king of Persia.
>
> —EZRA 6:14

> And they rose early in the morning, and went forth into the wilderness of Tekoa: and as they went forth, Jehoshaphat stood and said, Hear me, O Judah, and ye inhabitants of Jerusalem; Believe in the LORD your God, so shall ye be established; believe his prophets, so shall ye prosper.
>
> —2 CHRONICLES 20:20

The Jews were able to overcome the discouragement and opposition to the rebuilding of the temple and the walls of Jerusalem. They succeeded in rebuilding through the prophesying of these two prophets. They provided encouragement to rebuild, because it was the purpose of God for that generation. They were able to finish the work and prosper in what they were doing.

> And he sought God in the days of Zechariah, who had understanding in the visions of God: and as long as he sought the LORD, God made him to prosper.
>
> —2 CHRONICLES 26:5

Uzziah sought God and prospered. He had the assistance of Zechariah, who had understanding in the visions of God. Prophets can help us in our pursuit of God. Prophetic ministry awakens us to a realm where we can know the purpose and plans for our lives. They can be instrumental in our prosperity.

Uzziah had the advantage of having a prophet in his life. He was able to find God with the assistance of Zechariah the prophet. On the other hand we are at a disadvantage without the prophetic ministry.

> And the child Samuel ministered unto the LORD before Eli. And the word of the LORD was precious in those days; there was no open vision.
>
> —1 SAMUEL 3:1

Israel was at a disadvantage during the days when there was no open vision. They were living in apostasy and were constantly under the oppression of their enemies. God raised up the prophet Samuel to bring them deliverance.

Israel's prosperity began to change with the birth of Samuel. The word of the Lord began to come to Samuel, and he in turn began to raise the level of the prophetic in Israel. It was during this time that Israel experienced the blessing of David's kingdom and the prosperity under Solomon.

Companies of prophets and the school of the prophets were developed under Samuel's ministry. Prophets such as David, Gad, Nathan, Jeduthun, Heman, and Asaph were alive during this period. Even King Saul prophesied. Israel reached the zenith of its power during this time.

David established worship in Israel during this time, and the nation worshipped God and did not worship idols. His was a major change from the days of the judges when they continually worshipped idols.

> And the king made silver and gold at Jerusalem as plenteous as stones, and cedar trees made he as the sycamore trees that are in the vale for abundance.
> —2 CHRONICLES 1:15

This was the culmination of what started during the days of Samuel. This was a level of prosperity Israel had never seen before. Solomon departed from God, and Israel went back into idolatry. From that point forward prophets became the enemy. They were persecuted and rejected for challenging the immorality and idolatry of Israel.

We must not allow ourselves to reject or despise the prophetic ministry. Those who receive and embrace it will prosper, and those who oppose and reject it can find themselves in trouble. We need the prophetic advantage, and we will be blessed as we desire and covet to prophesy.

The Sevenfold Ministry of the Holy Spirit

I was recently ministering in South Africa. While I was having lunch at the waterfront, a rainbow appeared in sky and the Lord spoke these words to me: "I am empowering My church with a prophetic advantage by releasing the seven spirits of God to touch this generation. This anointing will equip, empower, and mobilize a new generation of global leaders with a prophetic advantage to influence every system of society with the kingdom message. This spirit of wisdom and revelation will increase in the earth exponentially. It will cause My people to be ten times better in wisdom, creativity, music, science, literature, and the arts just like the prophet Daniel. This company of believers will be known as the greater works generation. They will walk in a fullness of My Spirit just like My Son, Jesus."

> As for these four youths, God gave them knowledge and skill in all learning and wisdom, and Daniel had understanding in all [kinds of] visions and dreams. Now at the end of the time which the king had set for bringing [all the young men in], the chief of the eunuchs brought them before Nebuchadnezzar. And the king conversed with them, and among them all none was found like Daniel, Hananiah, Mishael, and Azariah; therefore they were assigned to stand before the king. And in all matters of wisdom and understanding concerning which the king asked them, he found them ten times better than all the [learned] magicians and enchanters who were in his whole realm.
>
> —DANIEL 1:17–20, AMP

Daniel had wisdom and revelation ten times better than the wise men of Babylon. He was a prototype of a generation that will penetrate society by a prophetic advantage. It was God's prophetic anointing on his life that made him ten times better. It gave him an advantage over the king and his magicians. He had understanding and wisdom in all matters. All means all. Whatever subject matter the king inquired of, Daniel had a supernatural endowment from heaven to answer.

I finished my lunch and returned to my hotel room. I opened the curtain, and there was another beautiful rainbow in the sky. I heard the Lord say, "I have brought you to the rainbow nation to unlock a rainbow of revelation regarding the sevenfold ministry of the Holy Spirit." He said, "Just like the rainbow has seven different colors but is one bow, the Holy Spirit has seven different characteristics but is one spirit. This is different than the nine gifts of the Spirit and nine fruit of the Spirit."

The centerpiece of the outpouring in the Book of Acts was the ability to prophesy, but it also made available an entire revelatory realm. God declares that He will pour out of His Spirit. This is the same Spirit that rested on Jesus and is described in the Book of Isaiah. Now after the resurrection Jesus has released the same seven spirits of God to remain in the church once again.

The Lord Jesus Christ is raising up a generation of sons who will be His expressed image in the earth. We will reflect the image and nature of Jesus. We will speak as He speaks and walk in power and authority of heaven just as He does. God is preparing a remnant who will have the Spirit without measure, a body of people who will have His in fullness. These believers will walk in the full life of the sevenfold Holy Spirit of God.

> And there between the throne and the four living creatures (beings) and among the elders [of the heavenly Sanhedrin] I saw a Lamb standing, as though it had been slain, with seven horns and with seven eyes, which are the seven Spirits of God [the sevenfold Holy Spirit] Who have been sent [on duty far and wide] into all the earth.
>
> —REVELATION 5:6, AMP

Notice in this passage of Scripture the seven Spirits of God have been sent into all the earth with the power and wisdom of God to govern this whole world. The Spirit of the Lord gives the king his skills to rule, a truth clearly seen in Christ's ministry (Luke 4:14).

In Isaiah 11:1–4 we can see clearly what the sevenfold Spirit of God is:

1. The spirit of the Lord or the fullness of the divine nature of God

2. The spirit of wisdom

3. The spirit of understanding

4. The spirit of counsel

5. The spirit of might

6. The spirit of knowledge

7. The spirit of the fear of the Lord

The seven distinct ministries of the Holy Spirit mentioned are thought by some to be the Old Testament counter reference to Revelation 4:5, revealing multiplicity of expression in the Holy Spirit's workings. This anointing is being released to give believers a prophetic advantage. Because the Spirit of God is upon us, just as Jesus did when He walked the earth, we will not judge after the sight of our eyes. We will have true spiritual vision.

God is raising up prophetic counselors who will not decide matters because of what they "think" they hear. They will tune in directly to the voice and judgments of the Lord and His righteousness. They will rely on the rule of God and the power of His spoken Word. The Holy Spirit will take ordinary people and demonstrate the fullness of His power and glory to world.

Those who become living epistles walking in the fullness of the sevenfold spirit of the Lord will have a prophetic advantage to judge not after the sight of natural eyes but from an anointing that will cause an acceleration in understanding.

The Lord is bringing forth a body of people to do what He does. There is a full-grown Jesus living inside of each of us. Jesus was a seed that went into the soil, and He wants a harvest of people who walk in the same dimension of spirit power that He did. Jesus was the firstborn of many brethren.

The anointing of God's government is the seven spirits of God. This anointing gave Jesus His skill to rule and make decisions by the Spirit.

The Sevenfold Spirit of God Expressed

> By means of these He has bestowed on us His precious and
> exceedingly great promises, so that through them you may
> escape [by flight] from the moral decay (rottenness and cor-
> ruption) that is in the world because of covetousness (lust and
> greed), and become sharers (partakers) of the divine nature.
>
> —2 PETER 1:4, AMP

The spirit of the Lord

The spirit of the Lord is coming upon the body of Christ to establish His government, dominion, and rule in us. Those who embody
this spirit will not only operate in the gifts of the Spirit but also
the manifest presence of the spirit of the Lord. The spirit of the
Lord will cause a greater expression of His nature and abilities to
be manifested in lives of believers. Let's look at how this will be
demonstrated.

The spirit of wisdom

Wisdom, or *chokmah* in Greek, means skill, to have good sense.[2]
It's the spirit of creativity, which was the ancient anointing present
when the Lord created the earth. Proverb 3:19 states that by wisdom
the Lord has created and founded the earth.

Wisdom is an abiding anointing. Wisdom will show us how to
create. This ancient anointing was God's servant working in the
creation of the world.

This prophetic anointing will help to access the invisible realm.
The invisible unseen realm is more real than the seen realm.
Creativity is the ability to see that which is waiting to exist.

Creativity can be defined as the ability to transcend traditional
ideas, rules, patterns, relationships, or the like, and to create mean-
ingful new ideas, forms, methods, interpretations, and so on. It is
originality and progressiveness. It is the process by which one utilizes

creative abilities. Some of the synonyms are originality, imagination, inspiration, ingenuity, inventiveness, and resourcefulness.

The Lord is pouring out His spirit of wisdom upon the body of Christ. Wisdom gives us creative and spiritual insight in every situation to know what to do, when to do it, and how to do it. Wisdom allowed Solomon to be a king, inventor, writer, scientist, and psalmist.

> And God gave Solomon exceptionally much wisdom and understanding, and breadth of mind like the sand of the seashore. Solomon's wisdom excelled the wisdom of all the people of the East and all the wisdom of Egypt. For he was wiser than all other men—than Ethan the Ezrahite, and Heman, Calcol, and Darda, the sons of Mahol. His fame was in all the nations round about. He also originated 3,000 proverbs, and his songs were 1,005. He spoke of trees, from the cedar that is in Lebanon to the hyssop that grows out of the wall; he spoke also of beasts, of birds, of creeping things, and of fish.
>
> —1 KINGS 4:29–33, AMP

The benefits of this anointing will give us an advantage in book writing, painting, plays, movie scripts, inventions, cures for diseases, and writing new songs.

I believe that the best is yet ahead. It had been said that Michael Jackson was one of greatest entertainers of our times, but I believe the best singer-songwriters are still in the earth. The Lord will anoint His people with this spirit of wisdom to create the greatest songs ever sung—songs that will penetrate hardness of hearts and change our generation. George Washington Carver asked the Lord for the secrets of the universe, but the Lord told him that He would give him revelation regarding the use of the peanut instead. He was one of the greatest scientists of modern times.[3]

Hebrews 11:7 says that Noah operated in wisdom and revelation to build an ark to save his generation. It had never rained before from the sky. He needed a prophetic advantage to look into the unseen realm and build an ark of safety for his family. The Lord gave him divine intelligence and specific instructions to create something that never existed before. Just as Noah did, the church will receive revelation from God through prophets and prophetic believers to prevail in our generation that will give them an advantage.

> Then the LORD spoke to Moses, saying: "See, I have called by name Bezalel the son of Uri, the son of Hur, of the tribe of Judah. And I have filled him with the Spirit of God, in wisdom, in understanding, in knowledge, and in all manner of workmanship, to design artistic works, to work in gold, in silver, in bronze, in cutting jewels for setting, in carving wood, and to work in all manner of workmanship."
>
> —EXODUS 31:1–5, NKJV

The spirit of understanding

This anointing gives one the power to see to the heart of the matter. It's the ability to interpret. It is the supernatural endowment abiding in the intellect, whereby it is elevated and enabled to understand spiritual truth with special clarity. It is having the ability to solve problems.

The prophet Daniel had supernatural insight into and interpretation of the plan of God for his generation and ages to come. He solved problems and riddles and encountered angels that gave him skill to understand mysteries of the kingdom (Dan. 9:22).

The spirit of counsel

The spirit of counsel gives strategy and the ability to devise the right course of action. The prophet Elijah had the counsel of the Lord to build an altar and place water upon it. Then he operated in the spirit of might to call down fire.

This ministry of the Spirit of God gives His people direction and guidance concerning God's mind and will.

Prophets are required to stand in the counsel of the Lord to hear the voice of God accurately and cause mankind to turn from evil. The premier anointing in the prophet's life should be conviction and the fear of the Lord.

> For who has stood in the counsel of the LORD, and has perceived and heard His word? Who has marked His word and heard it?...But if they had stood in My counsel, and had caused My people to hear My words, then they would have turned them from their evil way and from the evil of their doings.
>
> —JEREMIAH 23:18–22, NKJV

The word *counsel* is the Hebrew word *cowd*. Counsel or *cowd* refers to secret or private counsel, a family circle in which secrets are shared. It also refers to a session or a company of persons in (close deliberation) intimacy—close circle of friends, intimacy with God, to sit down together.[4]

The art of standing in the counsel of the revealer of secrets and mysteries must return to prophetic ministry. The term "standing before the Lord" means to wait attentively to hear the message that God wants to deliver. Prophets must spend time marking and perceiving the word of the Lord for many of the crises we face today. The Lord has counsel for the mother who has a homosexual son. The Lord has counsel for America's economy.

This is the anointing to counsel kings and heads of state and presidents.

Many are seeking networks, and the greatest network is that of the Father, the Son, the Holy Spirit, and you.

While in worship I had a vision of what appeared to be a heavenly council sitting at a long table. They were talking about mankind and the things of the earth. I heard the Holy Spirit say, "There are many strategies, plans, and solutions for the human plight, and I'm inviting a generation of people into My planning meetings.

There will be a generation of people on the earth who understand the counsel of My will."

The spirit of might

Elijah had boldness and confidence to face Ahab who was known as one of the wickedest kings in the earth. Elijah had stood in the counsel of the Lord and the spirit of might, as he declared that the people would see no rain on the land except by his word.

> And Elijah the Tishbite, of the inhabitants of Gilead, said to Ahab, "As the LORD God of Israel lives, before whom I stand, there shall not be dew nor rain these years, except at my word."
>
> —1 KINGS 17:1, NKJV

Elijah's bold proclamation caused an entire system of witchcraft to be destroyed but caused the hearts of the people to turn back to God.

The spirit of might refers to power and military strength, force, or the impetus to carry out the strategy of the Lord.

God is sovereign over the kingdoms of men, and He is leading history. It is the eternal Spirit who reveals to His prophets eternal secrets.

The spirit of knowledge

The spirit of knowledge is experience, living understanding, divine encounters, and personal relationship. It is the unveiling of the attributes of God by God Himself. It is more than informational facts. The spirit of knowledge paves the way for the spirit of the fear of the Lord.

> Now [when I was] in [my] thirtieth year, in the fourth month, in the fifth day of the month, as I was in the midst of captivity beside the river Chebar [in Babylonia], the heavens were opened and I saw visions of God. On the fifth day of the month, which was in the fifth year of King Jehoiachin's

captivity, the word of the Lord came expressly to Ezekiel the priest, the son of Buzi, in the land of the Chaldeans by the river Chebar; and the hand of the Lord was there upon him.

—EZEKIEL 1:1–3, AMP

Ezekiel is an example of a prophet who walked in the spirit of knowledge. He said he saw heaven open. First I would like to say that the Lord initiated the open heaven. Open heaven can be defined as a season when the supernatural invades the natural. It is when God gives an invitation to access the heavenly realm. It is an opening designed by God that starts in the third heaven where the throne of God is located, travels through the second heaven, and lands as an opening on the earth. This portal releases light and revelation.

When the heavens are opened:

1. We see visions of God. The experiential knowledge of God is released. Then He begins to reveal His attributes.

2. The word of the Lord comes expressly, clearly, unhindered, and with certainty. This kind of prophetic encounter is a mouth-to-mouth, word-for-word conversation. It doesn't need any interpretation.

3. The hand of God is upon us, and we will receive supernatural empowerment from God. The Holy Spirit is in the earth to empower us to overcome.

He is releasing keys that will allow the body of Christ to access our inheritance, which is in heavenly places. Prophets will carry mantles of revelation and power. Revelation is being given to cause complete agreement between the heavens and the earth. (See Ephesians 1:10.)

The spirit of truth is being released to prophets, allowing them to apprehend the heart of God and articulate with power and authority to this generation.

According to Webster's dictionary, *revelation* is "the act of disclosing or discovering to others what was before unknown to them."[5] It is the communication of truth to men by God or by His authorized agents—the prophet and apostles. The key to saving this end-time generation is that revelation must come from God!

The spirit of the fear of the Lord

The spirit of the fear of the Lord is reverential obedience. It brings the trembling and awe and tangible presence of the Lord. The fear of the Lord causes our spirit to feel clean and invigorated and has the ability to motivate our hearts in a powerful and sustained way. This anointing will grace us to make it our determined goal to be well pleasing to the Lord. The spirit of the fear of the Lord will awaken our hearts to a conscious awareness that He is watching, that He cares, and that He remembers so that He may reward us openly. (See Psalm 19:9; Proverbs 9:10; 2 Corinthians 5:9.)

Believers with a prophetic advantage will be equipped, activated, and released to penetrate the world with gospel of the kingdom. God is raising up a generation of believers who will operate in the fullness of His glory and power. Joel 2:28–29 speaks of a day when the Lord will pour out His Spirit on the sons and daughters, and as a result they all will prophesy. Truly an army is being raised up, and Jesus is calling for all of His troops to be adequately trained and equipped in the gifts of the Spirit. It is the purpose of this book not only to have scriptural teachings concerning the prophetic realm but also to advance God's people out of the realm of theory and bring them into a living, experiential reality of God's grace and power moving through them.

In times of uncertainty and turbulence the Lord has given me a mandate to raise up a company of believers who have confidence in

His sovereignty, a compass of righteousness in their hearts, and the word of the Lord in their mouths.

I wanted to start this book off with an understanding of the advantages of having an activated prophetic voice over our own lives and the body of Christ as well as what happens when there is no prophetic voice, so that you will begin to covet, or desire earnestly, the gift for your life. I wanted to start here so that your desire to have the word of the Lord in your life will be strengthened. I want you to be able to hunger after this first so that you will do whatever it takes to get in position to discern and sense the voice of the Lord for yourself. We cannot live out the call of God on our lives without the prophetic anointing being activated in our lives. We will not see change and breakthrough in our jobs, families, financial situations, health, and homes without it. We need a prophetic advantage.

Chapter 3

Prophets Are Builders

[Ye] are built upon the foundation of the apostles and prophets, Christ Jesus himself being the chief corner stone.

—EPHESIANS 2:20

For we are fellow workmen (joint promoters, laborers together) with and for God; you are God's garden and vineyard and field under cultivation, [you are] God's building. According to the grace (the special endowment for my task) of God bestowed on me, like a skillful architect and master builder I laid [the] foundation, and now another [man] is building upon it. But let each [man] be careful how he builds upon it, for no other foundation can anyone lay than that which is [already] laid, which is Jesus Christ (the Messiah, the Anointed One).

—1 CORINTHIANS 3:9–11, AMP

THE CHURCH IS the congregation of believers both locally and universally. Scripture uses a number of metaphors to describe the church and Christ's relationship with the church. It is the body, of which Jesus Christ is the head. It is a spiritual building in which Christ is both foundation and chief cornerstone, built also on the foundation that apostles and prophets lay.

A building is only as strong as the foundation upon which it is laid. Too many leaders are trying to build skyscraper churches on a hut foundation. If you try and build a church on anything expect the Lord Jesus Christ, it is destined to fall. A church must stand on the Lord Jesus Christ, or it doesn't stand at all. Prophets release prophetic utterances of the spirit in the local church that help establish the vision of the glorified and ascended Christ in the hearts and minds of the people.

The church is not a material building but a spiritual house built of living stones, which are people. The church is to be built as the habitation of God by the Spirit. Christ is building His church by the power of His Spirit through prophets and prophetic ministry. If the church is to grow into maturity, it must utilize the building anointing of prophets. To alleviate prophets from the building process of the church is to take away the key of knowledge, which is one of the most vital tools in building strong New Testament churches.

Many churches do not have the fullness of the Spirit because they are out of agreement with the Spirit's intentions and agenda for the church. Prophets are God's idea. He set them in the church secondarily after apostles. It is not possible to run a church organization or a ministry without direct leadership of the Holy Spirit in the daily flow of the church. Prophets and prophetic ministry are essential to the growth and maturity of the church because they have been gifted with an ability to hear wisdom and insight from God.

The primary directive of prophetic ministry is to cause believers to build their lives on the foundation of Christ. Prophets lay the foundation of Christ into the very nature and life of believers. Prophets build the foundation based upon God's purpose and destiny of each life. The revelation of the person, power, and work of Jesus Christ is the essence of prophetic ministry.

Fitted Together Into a Spiritual House

> In whom all the building fitly framed together groweth unto an holy temple in the Lord: in whom ye also are builded together for an habitation of God through the Spirit.
>
> —EPHESIANS 2:21–22

Synoikodomeō means to build together or with others, to put together or construct by building out of several things to build up one whole.[1]

The living stones are being gathered but not assembled. Prophets have an ability to hew, shape, and cut the stones through prophetic edification, exhortation, comfort, correction, and direction. Some of the stones have been burnt and broken by the trials of life. Let all things be done for the edification of the church. Everything we do as prophets in the church ought to be designed to build up, to encourage, and to strengthen God's people. The prophetic anointing has the ability to comfort the soul, exhort the body, and edify the spirit. The gathered stones must be hewn and measured to fit together in the corporate house. People must be built up and assembled in their proper place in the local church. Prophets help identify callings, gifts, talents, and assignments in the local church. Many times at the new member class graduation prophets prophesy over each graduate, giving them guidance and direction. This type of ministry helps activate and motivate the individual to find their part in the whole body.

> But he that prophesieth speaketh unto men to edification, and exhortation, and comfort.
> —1 Corinthians 14:3

Prophecy is for edification. We must not believe that all prophets do is tear down. Prophets and prophetic people also build. Prophets are builders. They help build people and churches. We need the building anointing of the prophet's ministry.

> And the elders of the Jews builded, and they prospered through the prophesying of Haggai the prophet and Zechariah the son of Iddo. And they builded, and finished it, according to the commandment of the God of Israel, and according to the commandment of Cyrus, and Darius, and Artaxerxes king of Persia.
> —Ezra 6:14

The building of the temple prospered through the prophesying of Haggai and Zechariah. The church is now the temple of the Lord.

Prophecy helped the leaders and people overcome discouragement and opposition. It was especially beneficial to the leaders Zerubbabel and Jeshua. Leaders need the edification of prophecy.

> And now, brethren, I commend you to God, and to the word of his grace, which is able to build you up, and to give you an inheritance among all them, which are sanctified.
>
> —ACTS 20:32

Prophets can minister grace to the hearers that builds them up. Grace can been defined as the ability of God to do something you could not do in your own strength. Prophets through the power of impartation can release a special anointing to complete an assignment given by God. I have seen the prophetic word release great encouragement in the lives of individuals and churches. I have seen leaders built up in faith through prophecy. Remember "faith comes by hearing, and hearing by the word of God" (Rom. 10:17).

The Church Is God's Building

> For we are labourers together with God: ye are God's husbandry, ye are God's building.
>
> —1 CORINTHIANS 3:9

The prophetic word is an indispensable tool for the building up of the church in faith and love for one another. Prophecy is for edification, exhortation, and comfort.

Exhortation is to incite, advise by words, to animate or give life to, to quicken, to make alive, to urge by arguments to a good deed or to any laudable (praiseworthy) conduct or course of action. It is also to warn, to caution, to set in motion, arouse, and stir up. Exhortation is the act of crying out, wooing, and calling near. The primary function of exhortation is to prompt and urge the church to draw near to God.

> And many other things in his exhortation preached he unto
> the people.
>
> —LUKE 3:18

Exhortation was prominent in the ministry of John the Baptist in calling Israel back to God. He encouraged a generation to repent because the kingdom was at hand.

> And Judas and Silas, being prophets also themselves, exhorted
> the brethren with many words, and confirmed them.
>
> —ACTS 15:32

Judas and Silas used their prophetic gifts to exhort and confirm the early church.

> Who, when he came, and had seen the grace of God, was glad,
> and exhorted them all, that with purpose of heart they would
> cleave unto the Lord.
>
> —ACTS 11:23

Prophets can see the grace, talents, and ability of God upon individuals and churches, and exhort them.

One of the functions of prophetic ministry is to see what the Lord has deposited in individuals and churches and draw it out of them through prophetic words and activations. Barnabas had a strong ministry of exhortation, and he is listed among the prophets and teachers at Antioch (Acts 13:1).

> Or he that exhorteth, on exhortation: he that giveth, let him
> do it with simplicity; he that ruleth, with diligence; he that
> sheweth mercy, with cheerfulness.
>
> —ROMANS 12:8

Prophets can have strong gifts of exhortation. They can exhort through prophecy, singing, preaching, and teaching. Exhortation is a powerful tool in building churches.

Prophecy also confirms. To confirm means to make firm or strengthen, to make valid by formal approval, to prove as true that which is doubtful or certain, to make secure. It means to establish, to fix, strengthen, to set, to make firm or solid, and to cause to stand.

Prophets confirm believers in their destinies. "Confirm" is the Greek word *epistērizō*, meaning to render firmer, strengthen more, or to establish besides.[2] Prophets minister strength to the churches. Their words firm up believers.

> And he went through Syria and Cilicia, confirming the churches.
>
> —Acts 15:41

Churches need confirmation. Churches need the assurance that they are walking in the will of God. This is a key to strong churches. God confirms people and churches through the ministry of the prophets.

God's Blueprint

Every builder must have a blueprint. You cannot build without a blueprint. Prophets are spiritual architects. They receive revelation through the Spirit that gives them the blueprints for building. God is a builder (Heb. 11:10). He builds through His ministry gifts, including prophets.

> According to all that I shew thee, after the pattern of the tabernacle, and the pattern of all the instruments thereof, even so shall ye make it.
>
> —Exodus 25:9

> And look that thou make them after their pattern, which was
> shewed thee in the mount.
>
> —EXODUS 25:40

Moses was told to build the tabernacle after the pattern he received on the mount. Prophets receive patterns. They receive blueprints by the Spirit. They help build by revelation.

> Through wisdom is an house builded; and by understanding
> it is established.
>
> —PROVERBS 24:3

Prophets have wisdom for building. They can target the hindrances to building. Churches must be built and established through wisdom and understanding.

> All this, said David, the LORD made me understand in writing
> by his hand upon me, even all the works of this pattern.
>
> —1 CHRONICLES 28:19

David received the pattern to build the temple by the Spirit. Solomon built the temple based on this pattern. Patterns are important. I have been asked many times by emerging prophets what are the patterns used for building in the local churches. Below you will find patterns and strategies given me from the Book of Revelation for building the church.

Pattern can be defined as a model proposed for imitation. Jesus's messages to the seven churches provide patterns, methods, and strategies for ministering to the church. Although Jesus was speaking specifically to the seven churches, these truths are relevant and applicable today. Jesus addresses seven characteristics and traits of the universal church. Seven represents the number of completion and perfection. Jesus gives a complete picture of the issues facing the church at large and gives perfect answers and solutions needed.

The structure of the letters falls into an eightfold pattern that prophets can use for ministering in the local church. First I will list the pattern, and then I would like to look at each church individually, pointing out the methods used for ministering as well as the characteristic of each church that is comparable to the church today.

The Prophetic Pattern

- Jesus gave a commission to each messenger, senior leader, or set man.

- Jesus named each church and its geographical location.

- Jesus revealed a character description of Himself.

- Jesus gave a commendation to each church.

- Jesus spoke to a specific area that needed correction.

- Jesus gave instructions for correction and momentum.

- Jesus gave the twofold challenge to hear and overcome.

- Jesus gave the promise.

The commission to the senior leader

The Lord gives a commission to the messenger or leader of the church. Jesus demonstrated that He honors and does not bypass the authority of the senior leader. The senior leader has the grace to lead the church. He will judge and interpret the prophetic ministry. He has the responsibility to determine when a prophetic word should be executed in the church.

When ministering in local church, prophets should prepare for ministry by praying for the senior leader. Prayer will allow the prophet's heart to be enlarged and receive the Lord's heart and mind for the senior leader. During these times the Lord will reveal how He feels about the senior leader, many times imparting His emotions for the senior leader.

When prophets declare the emotions of God, a tangible presence is released imparting that emotion in the people. This will cause the people to see the senior leader through the eyes of God, releasing new honor and respect for the senior leader.

Prophets should never take over or elevate themselves above the senior leader. They should help cultivate the vision confirming the mission and plans of the leader.

Before my ministry time with a church I always ask the leader for a copy of the church vision. Then I spend quality time praying over the vision. During this prayer time I ask the Lord questions such as:

- Is this the heavenly vision given by Your spirit?

- Is this leader on task, and if not, how can I help direct them to original vision?

- Is this a direction that should be given publicly or privately?

- Do I have favor with this pastor to deliver such a word?

- In what area does the leader need encouragement?

- What is the ultimate thing You want to accomplish during this time of meeting?

Distinction given to each church

Like snowflakes and fingerprints every local church is unique. Jesus addressed each church by name signifying the individual nature, character, and destiny of the church. The natural environment of the seven churches played a prophetic role in pointing out their spiritual conditions. It's important to understand the geographical location of a church. Many times when the Lord speaks, He addresses the church and the city as a whole, the culture and community. Local climate and the spiritual atmosphere affect the belief system of a region and congregation. A church located in a big city faces different strongholds than a church in a rural area. Prophets must discern the spiritual atmosphere of church culture to minister effectively.

Jesus's nature is in His name

Jesus reveals a character description of Himself. Prophets are representatives of the Lord. God has given prophets to speak on His behalf. The Lord doesn't just want to reveal information about Himself; He also wants to manifest Himself. Prophetic ministry is a ministry that feels and releases the divine heart of God. God is revealed in His name. Prophets should study the divine names of God. This will enhance their articulation of the character, attributes, activities, emotions, and will of God. A proclamation about God causes the God of that proclamation to fill the atmosphere. The words of a prophet can activate a consciousness and awareness of the presence of God. Sometimes He will reveal Himself as Jehovah Rapha, the God who heals, and a tremendous anointing is present during the ministry time for healing.

The commendation

Jesus gave commendation for what was being done correctly in the church. Prophets should discipline themselves to applaud and salute leaders for what is being done effectively by the leadership team. The prophet's message should strengthen. There are two major complaints that I hear from senior leaders who pastor prophets: 1) immature prophets only discern the danger with no plan of action to avert, and 2) immature prophets only see doom and gloom and not the redemptive purpose of God.

The area of correction

When ministering in a church, the prophet should have a specific area that the Lord has revealed that needs correction. Jesus gave each church a specific place of constructive criticism. It's important at this stage to determine if the message should be given to the senior leader publicly or privately. Most correction words should be judged by leadership before delivery over the congregation. The interpretation and application of the prophetic word is at the discretion of the senior leader. The senior leader must filter the partial, progressive, and conditional part of the prophecy.

The instruction for correction

When prophets give a word of correction, there should always be clear instructions and solutions for correction. If the Lord hasn't given you a solution to the problem revealed by your revelatory gift, wait until He does. Five out of the seven churches received words of correction, but the counsel was always the same—repent. Repentance is one of predominant messages that prophets promote. Repentance was only the first step to align with the instruction of the Lord. Each church was given specific instructions to follow. Prophets carry an anointing that brings the convicting power of the Holy Spirit, causing the human heart to turn back to the Lord.

The twofold challenge

1. This admonishment was given to all seven churches: "he that hath an ear, let him hear" (Rev. 2:7, 11, 17, 29; 3:6, 13, 22). This speaks to the spiritual dullness of hearing and obeying the instructions of the Lord. Prophets have an ability to break spiritual deafness, awakening the spiritual ear to hear and causing the heart to understand the instructions of the Lord. Hearing is not enough. The word of the Lord must be obeyed.

2. Jesus's divine challenge was for the churches to overcome. Prophets should deliver messages that empower

the church to overcome. Prophets should encourage and provide keys to conquer obstacles and opposition to victory in the life of the church.

The promise

There is a reward for obeying the instructions of the Lord. The Lord promised if you obey the prophets, you will prosper. The Lord always comes with His rewards with Him. Prophets must always seal the message with comfort and hope.

The Challenges of the Seven Churches

The church today struggles with some of the same issues the church in the first century struggled with. Jesus uses His prophets to be the voice crying out for transformation and change. Jesus's prophetic message to these churches provides valuable guidelines a prophet can use to build the church. Let's take a look at the seven different types of churches and the unique challenges they faced.

The church in Ephesus: the apostolic church (Rev. 2:1–7)

Ephesus was a fighting, hard-working church. It had intolerance for doctrinal impurity and was one of the leading training and sending churches of its time. But this church had lost its first love. They were busy doing the work of the Lord, yet they were not in relationship with the Lord of the work. Christ was no longer first. They were putting the church first with its programs, services, and ministries. They were structured, but union with Christ had been lost. Their service had become mechanical. This church had a form of godliness but denied the power. Prophets have an ability to preach messages that ignite a passion for Christ. They deal with compromise and complacency. Prophets exhort the church to make God first. They create access to the Father by promoting life in the Spirit above ritualistic works.

The church in Smyrna: the persecuted church (Rev. 2:8–11)

Smyrna is a picture of what every church should be—a dynamic witness to Christ and His truth no matter the trial or temptation. I had the honor of ministering in a church that had suffered persecution because of the gospel in the Middle East. There was an awesome presence to encourage and strengthen the believers in the faith. God flooded them with His tangible presence.

A prophet's message to a Smyrna church should be one of encouragement, following Jesus's example in this passage. Jesus said to them that they should not be afraid. He told them to be faithful and that they should endure their trials and tribulation, knowing that He had a crown of life waiting for them.

The church in Pergamos: the corrupted church that is married to the world (Rev. 2:12–17)

This church participated in worldly functions. The church and its members allowed worldly activities to take place in the church. The church began to baptize and accept members who had not repented and turned from the world to Christ. The church allowed false teaching and preaching. This just described much of the Western church culture. The method of ministry to this type of church can be found in the depiction of Christ to this church—"he which hath the sharp sword with two edges" (Rev. 2:12).

Prophets are like the two-edge sword in the mouth God. The Lord will give them a prophetic word to judge and separate the mixture of worldliness out of the church. Hebrews 4:12 says, "The word of God is living and active. Sharper than any double-edged sword, it penetrates even to dividing soul and spirit, joints and marrow; it judges the thoughts and attitudes of the heart" (NIV).

It's not enough to prophesy and proclaim. Prophets must be skilled in the Word to minister messages of sanctification and separation to the church. It is God's Word that is quick and powerful that brings conviction to the human heart. The Lord will raise up prophets to cry out against unrighteousness and the sins of people in the church. Holiness and righteousness are standard messages that every prophet should use to prick the conscience of believers and bring transformation.

The church in Thyatira: the morally compromising and corrupt church (Rev. 2:18–29)

Thyatira was a city known for its drunken socials and immoral parties. Many believers were putting their social acceptance before God. This church was tolerating false teaching, seduction, fornication, and idolatry in the church.

Prophets have an ability to identify idols in the heart. Idols can be defined as anything that a person puts first in his life. The church was allowing a false prophetess to seduce the servants of the Lord. One of the major demonic spirits that prophets have to contend with is the spirit of Jezebel. Romans 12:2 states that we should not be conformed to the ways of the world but be transformed by the renewing of our minds. In order to reach and influence the world, Christians do not have to be like the world.

The church in Sardis: the church has influence but is dead (Rev. 3:1–6)

This type of church focuses on activities and not Christ. They focused on formalism and ritualism. This church had become a place of social services and man-made activities. Jesus said it was void of spiritual life and energy. This church is parallel to many church organizations today. The works of these organizations do not have the Spirit of God and His power in them. Prophets are needed in churches like this because they give voice to the present movement of God. They challenge the status quo, provoking believers to hunger and thirst after God. They make it clear that what is honorable before men is detestable before God (Luke 16:15).

The church in Philadelphia: the faithful and alive church (Rev. 3:7–13)

Jesus did not have a complaint or correction for this church. He had only praise and commendation. As a prophet I use this church as a measuring tool for other churches. This church was steadfast in declaring the gospel. They used open-door evangelism and missions to reach people for Christ. The Lord had set an open door, and they took advantage of each opportunity.

The church in Laodicea: the lukewarm, indifferent church (Rev. 3:14–22)

The Laodicean church clearly mirrors many of the attributes of today's church. We have become self-sufficient and callous, drifting far from our devotion to Christ. Jesus said that this church was neither hot nor cold but lukewarm. Lukewarm can be defined as mildly warm, tepid, lacking conviction or enthusiasm, indifferent. This church, like many churches today, confused prosperity and material blessings with spirituality and spiritual blessings. Jesus's assessment of this church was that they were wretched, miserable, poor, blind, and naked (v. 17). This church was in deep self-deception. They felt rich and in need of nothing. They measured themselves by their own idea of righteousness and not the righteousness of Christ. Prophets have a God-given ability to see spiritual truths. They are to be the eye salve to the body of Christ. The nature and purpose of prophets and prophetic ministry is to open the eyes of the spiritually blind so they may see the reality of God in the realm of the spirit.

> According to the grace of God which is given unto me, as a wise masterbuilder, I have laid the foundation, and another buildeth thereon. But let every man take heed how he buildeth thereupon.
>
> —1 CORINTHIANS 3:10

Prophets must learn to build in sequence as wise master builders. A master builder is an architect, the superintendent in the erection of buildings. Prophets are not called to minister every revelation and truth in every church. You may not have the authority to minister to every problem discerned by your gift in the church. Jesus told His disciples, "I still have many things to say to you, but you cannot bear them now" (John 16:12, NKJV). Prophets make the mistake of trying to minister all of their revelations and bring correction to every problem discerned by their gift to the church in one visit. Based on the spiritual level of the church some prophetic revelations are too much for believers to bear. Prophets must take care not to minister above believers' levels of comprehension. Prophets must use wisdom, or as the apostle Paul admonishes, "Let every man take heed how he buildeth thereupon. For other foundation can no man lay than that is laid, which is Jesus Christ" (1 Cor. 3:10–11). "Take heed" comes from the Greek word *blepō*. It means "to consider, contemplate, to look at, to weigh carefully, examine."[3] This definition give the connotation of to *investigate*, which means to "carry out a systematic or formal inquiry to discover and examine the facts of…so as to establish the truth."[4] One of the major roles of prophets is to establish the church in present truth. The above-mentioned seven churches were in different locations each exhibiting different characteristics and levels of understanding. Asking questions is a major way to gauge the spiritual level of each church. The apostle Paul used the strategy of asking questions while upgrading the believers in Ephesus. (See Acts 19:1–3.) Asking questions will provide the prophet with insight as to which area should be the focus that will bring upgrade and breakthrough to the church. Asking questions will allow the prophet to determine their measure of authority. There are times when you are invited to introduce the prophetic and other times to bring instruction and correction in specific areas of the church. The senior leader of the house determines your measure of authority.

Chapter 4

The Creative Force of Prophecy

Let all the earth fear the Lord [revere and worship Him]; let all the inhabitants of the world stand in awe of Him. For He spoke, and it was done; He commanded, and it stood fast.

—PSALM 33:8–9, AMP

ONE OF THE greatest gifts the Lord has given prophets is the ability to create and build with their words. Words spoken in the right setting can bring forth life and healing to the human heart. Proverb 25:11 states, "Like apples of gold in settings of silver is a word spoken in right circumstances" (NAS). It takes only one word fitly spoken to a hurting soul to introduce or, in some cases, reintroduce Jesus Christ into his life and circumstance.

People are controlled with words. Human dignity is restored with words. Love is communicated through words, and our worlds are framed and created by words. Many believe that prophets are called to root up and tear down—and that is a vital part of the prophet's ministry—but the ability to build and create is also a vital function of the prophetic office. So many lives are dark, void, and without hope, purpose, or form. One God-empowered word from a prophet can bring light, structure, and fulfillment.

The first words God said was "let there be light" or "light be." (See Genesis 1:3.) God was not only foretelling light; His words were also creating light. Our first devotion as prophets should be to release light and expose darkness. It is time to bring restoration not devastation.

I found that it takes less effort to root up and tear down, but it takes love, patience, and wisdom to plant and build. Because I had a strong deliverance background in the initial stages of developing my prophetic gift, all I wanted to do was identify the devil and get him out without any concern for the human soul. I would accurately identify the problem without giving the solution. Prophets must mature in their gift to give solutions or what I call prophetic prescriptions. Prophets must not give blanket prophecy but really listen to the Holy Spirit regarding the condition of each human soul. True prophetic ministry imparts grace and truth that sets people free, showing them the way out of their sin and on to higher levels of spiritual maturity.

> In the beginning God created the heaven and the earth.
>
> —GENESIS 1:1

The Hebrew word here for "create" is *bara'*. It means to form, to fashion, to shape, to create.[1] It carries the idea of carving or cutting out. This suggests that creating is similar to sculpturing. *Bara'* is a word that describes both creating by bringing into existence and creating by fashioning existing matter into something new.[2]

Ezekiel 37 gives us an excellent picture of the condition of human souls in many of our churches and society. This chapter shows the power and the creative of force of prophecy. It shows how words spoken by a prophet can bring life where death has been and fresh strength where a person has been dry and weary.

Ezekiel was empowered with a creative force as a prophetic voice to bring hope, redemption, and restoration. Let's take a closer look at this chapter.

The Hand of the Lord

> The hand of the LORD was on me, and he brought me out by the Spirit of the LORD and set me in the middle of a valley; it was full of bones.
>
> —EZEKIEL 37:1, NIV

Prophets must realize that we are not called to everyone or everywhere. The hand of the Lord will lead you to the specific place you are assigned. The hand of the Lord set the prophet. *Set* means to be placed or fixed by appointment, agreement, and authority. It means to arrange, to put in a certain place, post, or position. When you are set in place by the hand of the Lord, you are given the authority of the kingdom to meet any challenge. You can rely on the grace of God to accomplish the assignment and not your own abilities. The hand of the Lord represents supernatural empowerment of the Holy Spirit that comes upon you, the prophet, to be the voice of change.

Set in the midst of the valley

The valley is the Lord's training ground for every prophet. The valley represents a place of obscurity and hiddenness. The valley also represents a low place. The Lord will prepare the prophet in small, valleylike places. This will develop humility and a servant heart.

The hand of the Lord positioned the prophet right in the middle of the valley of dry bones. Prophets should be set in a position to identify with and have compassion on those they minister to. One misconception regarding the prophet's ministry is that we deliver the word of the Lord by pointing out every fault that needs to be corrected and then we return to our cave. The Holy Spirit is called a helper, and those who prophesy by the Spirit will always be looking for ways to help and not just to stand aloof and criticize.

The Prophetic Survey

He led me back and forth among them, and I saw a great many bones on the floor of the valley, bones that were very dry.

—Ezekiel 37:2, NIV

Survey means to examine as to the condition, situation, or value. It also means to collect data, to appraise, to view or consider comprehensively. Here we see how the Lord led the prophet back and forward to take a survey, investigating the place of assignment. In order to be effective with creating change, prophets must view people, churches, and society from the Lord's perspective. Prophets must have a clear vision from the Lord of the height, width, and depth of their assignment. The surveillance allowed the prophet Ezekiel to see the scope of the task ahead. The Lord led him back and forth among them. Prophets will be known by the participation in the church and not the separation from the situation or church. Jesus was touched with the feelings of our infirmities, and likewise, prophets need to learn how to identify with the people they have been assigned to.

The Prophetic Questions

> He asked me, "Son of man, can these bones live?" I said, "Sovereign LORD, you alone know."
> —EZEKIEL 37:3, NIV

The prophet did not presume he knew how to function in this assignment. One of the biggest enemies to the prophet's ministry is presumption. Presumption can be defined as having an attitude that is arrogant and overconfidence in one's abilities. It's taking an idea that is true and often used as the basis for other ideas, although it is not known for certain. Prophets should always make sure we're not taking liberties that have not been given to us by the Lord.

In the early 1990s at Crusaders Church I was leading the prophetic team during the Friday night prophetic service. One night my good friend in ministry who had been suffering with sickle cell anemia walks in. I immediately beckon her to come to the front for ministry. I begin to prophesy the word of the Lord from Psalm 118:17: "You shall not die but live and declare the works of the Lord." I said it with all the love and prophetic authority I thought I had at the time. The very next week I attended her funeral, or as some Christians say, her homegoing celebration. I was completely devastated. When I inquired of the Lord as to what happened, He said that I was operating out of presumption. I gave a personal prophecy based on head knowledge of a scriptural truth without having the revelation quickened to my heart by the Holy Spirit for her situation. I should have inquired of the Lord first to know His heart toward my friend.

Prophetic questions help prophets avoid presumption. They prompt the prophet's awareness of the will of God for their specific assignment.

You See Dry Bones but I See an Army

> Then he said to me, "Prophesy to these bones and say to them, 'Dry bones, hear the word of the LORD! This is what the Sovereign LORD says to these bones: I will make breath enter you, and you will come to life. I will attach tendons to you and make flesh come upon you and cover you with skin; I will put breath in you, and you will come to life. Then you will know that I am the Lord.'"
>
> —EZEKIEL 37:4–6, NIV

The prophet must inquire of the Lord for the method of ministry to be used in the assignment. There are times when prophets preach or teach, but for this case the Lord said to prophesy to dry bones. Every prophet will have to pass the dry bones test. This test is the recalibration of sight. If the prophet passes the test, he or she will no longer see from their human perspective (the dry bones) but will see through eyes of faith and will bring the eternal perspective (the army).

It's important that the dry bones hear the prophetic word. The Lord told the prophet what to prophesy, but it's important that the bones hear. In this case they must hear and obey the word of the Lord. Prophets can ensure that bones are hearing by speaking words that are easy to understand. First Corinthians 14:9 states, "So likewise ye, except ye utter by the tongue words easy to be understood, how shall it be known what is spoken? for ye shall speak into the air." Many prophets' messages can be so confusing that you need a special decoder to determine the message. The prophetic message should be clear, definite, and distinct. The ultimate goal of the prophetic message should be that people listen, believe, and take action. The bones have a responsibility to respond and obey. This is an act of the free will. Prophets should never usurp a person's right to choose to obey the word of the Lord. This could lead to manipulation and control.

There is a progression and orderly process to seeing a people or nation restored. The Lord creates and builds in sequence and by patterns—first the blade, the ear, and then the corn. The Lord commanded the prophet to prophesy to the bones, sinews, flesh, skin, and then the breath. In the design of the human body, first sinews are laid to join the bones together; then flesh is laid to cover them, fill up all vacancies, and form muscles to make the bones capable of motion. The skin is laid to hold everything together and provide identification.

Many times as prophets we can prophesy out of sequence. I have found that a prophecy given out of sequence can become a stumbling block instead of a blessing. A stumbling block is something that obstructs motion. In the original Hebrew text it had the connotation of an individual whose ankles could not support their weight, thus they would constantly stumble and fall. If a person is struggling with pride and rebellion, they shouldn't be given words regarding worldwide ministry.

The creative constructive power of a prophet requires skill and patience.

God instructs the prophet to speak words that sculpt and shape much like the Genesis account of the creation of man.

1. The prophet had to prophesy to the bones. The bones represent something that was once alive. They represent a former life that was once alive but is now dead.

2. The prophet had to prophesy to the sinews. The sinews of the human body are the source of strength, power, and vigor. It is a piece of tough fibrous tissue uniting muscle to bone or bone to bone. Sinews represent the core of an individual—their morals, values, and belief systems—everything that holds a person together. The prophetic word has the ability to deal with deep-rooted issues in the innermost being. These words given by a prophet bring inner healing in places no other form of ministry can reach. Because these are eternal words spoken from an eternal Spirit, they are designed to bring forth resurrection life.

3. He prophesied to the flesh, which represents the carnal nature. These are thoughts and desires driven by the lust of the flesh, lust of the eyes, and the pride of life. Heaven and hell can manifest in our human desires. The lust of the flesh is natural appetites or desires all humans have. Prophets can minister words that lead to the path of holiness and righteousness. The lust of the eyes is the desire to have things of the world as necessities. The pride of life can be defined as having a success spirit seeking position, power, and prestige as a status symbol. Prophetic ministry releases a grace to align your desires to seek the kingdom above the things of the world. Proverbs 29:18 says, "Where there is no prophecy the people cast off restraint" (RSV).

4. The prophet spoke to the skin. The skin holds everything together. It is your personal identity. No one knows human beings like the Lord. He knows

what purpose each individual was created to fulfill. Everyone's skin is different; we have black, white, old, and young skin. Prophets reveal the unique call and purpose for every living soul.

They Came Together Bone to Bone

So I prophesied as I was commanded. And as I was prophesying, there was a noise, a rattling sound, and the bones came together, bone to bone. I looked, and tendons and flesh appeared on them and skin covered them, but there was no breath in them.

—EZEKIEL 37:7–8, NIV

Prophets have the ability to speak power-filled words that cause everyone to find their place in the army God. Here we see that the dry, useless, and disjointed bones began to come alive and unite— with the toe bone connected to the foot bone, and the foot bone connected to the anklebone, and the anklebone connected to the leg bone. I believe as prophets our prophetic ministry should point every member of the body to their proper place of function. Paul tells us in 1 Corinthians 12:18–21 that "God has set the members, each one of them, in the body just as He pleased.... There are many members, yet one body. And the eye cannot say to hand, 'I have no need of you'" (NKJV). The principle here is that everyone has a membership ministry in the body of Christ. Some function as the hand to serve, and some function as the eye to see, but everyone is important. True prophetic ministry will cause each member of the whole body to be joined and knitted together.

The Breath of God

The breath of God gives new life to the hopeless and resurrection to the dead. Hopelessness had gripped Israel. Hopelessness is an awful feeling. When people become hopeless, they become dejected, demoralized, and desperate. Hopelessness can make you feel like you're in a no-win situation. The command from God to prophesy infused the prophet with the creative force of God's divine nature. Prophetic words spoken by mature prophets contain within themselves the seed of God's divine nature, His life-giving nature.

The Holy Spirit is the source of life. The Holy Spirit will empower the prophet to speak words that break the power of death, releasing hope and new life. True prophetic ministry will create roads and access to new beginnings and fresh starts in a person life.

I was ministering in a church in Indiana and spoke over this one man regarding his position in the church and how the Lord wanted to use him. The Lord showed me this man kneeling by his bed praying for his pastor. Later I got a letter from his wife testifying that he had never done anything like that before, but in obedience to the prophetic word he got on his knees the next day to pray for his pastor. This act of obedience to the word of the Lord released an anointing on him to pray for his wife, which brought tremendous reconciliation and healing in their marriage. He wanted to minister to his wife and pray for his pastor, but he just didn't know how. The prophetic word gave him access and confidence to do what was already in his heart.

The Four Winds

> Then he said to me, "Prophesy to the breath; prophesy, son of man, and say to it, 'This is what the Sovereign Lord says: Come, breath, from the four winds and breathe into these slain, that they may live.'" So I prophesied as he commanded me, and breath entered them; they came to life and stood up on their feet—a vast army.
>
> —Ezekiel 37:9–10

The winds are connected to God and His supremacy and authority over His creation. The four winds connected together represent the totality of God's sovereign dominion. The prophet announces and demonstrates God's comprehensive power over life and death. There is coming a new generation of prophets who will not only speak the word of the Lord but will also demonstrate the power of the Lord so that our faith will not be in the wisdom of men but in the power of God.

> Then he said to me: "Son of man, these bones are the whole house of Israel. They say, 'Our bones are dried up and our hope is gone; we are cut off.' Therefore prophesy and say to them: 'This is what the Sovereign LORD says: O my people, I am going to open your graves and bring you up from them; I will bring you back to the land of Israel. Then you, my people, will know that I am the LORD, when I open your graves and bring you up from them. I will put my Spirit in you and you will live, and I will settle you in your own land. Then you will know that I the LORD have spoken, and I have done it, declares the LORD.'"
>
> —EZEKIEL 37:11–14, NIV

One of the primary directives of prophetic ministry is to help restore the image of God in the earth. Restoration in every dimension of human experience is at the heart of the gospel. It is woven through all Scripture and must be at the forefront of our ministry truth. The vision of the dry bones demonstrates the restorative power of prophecy. It is a picture of the recovery of men from their spiritual death and corruption—a parable of the way in which prophecy given by the command of God has the ability to resurrect any person's life. Through His life-giving Spirit God can take all of the fragmented pieces of your life and put them back together again. God used the tool of prophecy to cause these people to be brought up from their hopeless, spiritually dead condition and made them live by the power of the Holy Ghost.

Chapter 5

Character in the Prophetic Ministry

But thou hast fully known my doctrine, manner of life,
purpose, faith, longsuffering, charity, patience…

—2 Timothy 3:10

PROPHETS AND PROPHETIC people must walk in love, humility, and purity. Whenever we talk about character we are referring to your personality, attitude, and behavior patterns. Doctrine, gifting, and character all work together.

Make Your Calling and Election Sure

And beside this, giving all diligence, add to your faith virtue; and to virtue knowledge; and to knowledge temperance; and to temperance patience; and to patience godliness; and to godliness brotherly kindness; and to brotherly kindness charity. For if these things be in you, and abound, they make you that ye shall neither be barren nor unfruitful in the knowledge of our Lord Jesus Christ. But he that lacketh these things is blind, and cannot see afar off, and hath forgotten that he was purged from his old sins. Wherefore the rather, brethren, give diligence to make your calling and election sure: for if ye do these things, ye shall never fall.

—2 Peter 1:5–10

The call to the prophetic ministry requires a process of maturing. Prophets are called, trained, and commissioned.

There are several points I want to draw from these verses. Notice that we are to give all diligence in developing our character. Our character will determine the level of revelation and power the Lord will entrust to us. Development of character gives you the capacity to carry the authority of kingdom. The verses mention virtue, knowledge, temperance, patience, godliness, brotherly kindness, and charity (love). Notice that knowledge is included. I believe ignorance can be a character issue. True prophets should have knowledge, especially knowledge of the Word of God.

Secondly notice that he who lacks these things is blind (v. 9). Lack of character development will result in blindness. There is no way you can be effective in the prophetic ministry with blindness in your life.

Thirdly notice the way we make our calling and election sure. Prophets have a calling from heaven. How do we confirm this calling? The answer is by developing our character with all diligence. A good tree produces good fruit, and a bad tree cannot produce good fruit.

> Who hath saved us, and called us with an holy calling, not according to our works, but according to his own purpose and grace, which was given us in Christ Jesus before the world began.
>
> —2 TIMOTHY 1:9

The call of God is a holy calling and requires godly character. On the other hand false prophets are known by their fruit (bad character). This fruit includes lust, greed, covetousness, and pride.

> But as he which hath called you is holy, so be ye holy in all manner of conversation.
>
> —1 PETER 1:15

Prophets were called holy men. Holy men spoke as the Holy Ghost moved them.

The Call of the Prophet

The principles for understanding the process of the prophet's call can be found in Jeremiah 1:4–18. Let's examine these principles.

The call of God is eternal.

> Before I formed you in the womb I knew you...
>
> —JEREMIAH 1:5, NIV

Your calling is God's idea, and it is His purpose for your life. The call of God for your life originated in eternity, and it proceeded from His heart not from your will or imagination or from anyone else's will or imagination. The call of God started in your life before you were conceived in your mother's womb, and it will continue throughout eternity.

It is God who does the calling.

> I sanctified you; I ordained you...
>
> —JEREMIAH 1:5, NKJV

You do not call yourself, appoint yourself, of set yourself apart to anything; neither can anyone else call you to anything. It is God who sanctifies you, calls you, and ordains you. While it is God who calls and sanctifies, prophets should be confirmed and commissioned by a local church.

God chooses the field where your assignment will be fulfilled.

> I ordained you a prophet to the nations.... See, I have this day set you over the nations and over the kingdoms...
>
> —JEREMIAH 1:5, 10 NKJV

You may have a call to a neighborhood, a city, a county, a state, a nation, or the nations, but you must not choose your own field of service. When you attempt to choose your field, you are probably looking at what is in it for you. When God chooses your field, it is all about His kingdom. Do you want "mine" or "thine"? The anointing in your life will work effectively only in the field of God's calling on your life.

God appoints you to an office according to His will and purpose for your life.

> I ordained you a prophet...
>
> —JEREMIAH 1:5, NKJV

Positions and titles mean absolutely nothing without the anointing from God to function and produce fruit. Positions and titles without the anointing become the vain imaginations of those who lust for power and prestige.

God challenges what you see as your inadequacies.

> Do not say, "I am a youth..."
>
> —JEREMIAH 1:7, NKJV

There will always be feelings of inadequacy that rise up in your mind. The Lord will empower you to do and say whatever He commands.

God challenges your fears.

> Do not be afraid of their faces...
>
> —JEREMIAH 1:8, NKJV

There will always be fears that rise to eliminate faith. The Lord is with you to deliver you.

God chooses your message.

> Whatever I command you, you shall speak.... To root out and to pull down, to destroy and to throw down, to build and to plant.
>
> —JEREMIAH 1:7, 10, NKJV

You must discipline yourself to stay on the course of the message God has given to you in His call on your life.

God recalibrates how you see.

> What do you see?
>
> —JEREMIAH 1:11, NKJV

The almond tree was known as "the waker," alert and watching diligently for the opportunity to bloom and produce fruit.

The Lord was ready to perform His Word, and Jeremiah was to be alert and watching for the fulfillment of such a word. The Lord was stirring action that would come in response to the actions of His people, and Jeremiah was to be prepared for the fulfillment of such action.

You will see yourself as a willing, alert, and diligent participant in the purpose of God.

God makes you what He wants you to be.

> Behold, I have made you this day...
>
> —JEREMIAH 1:18, NKJV

Jeremiah was made to be a bulwark of strength against the system of the world.

You will be formed to be whatever God has designed you to be in this world, and you will reveal the strength of the Lord against every anti-Christ spirit and system.

The Call to Love

God is love. Love is His nature. Love may be the most powerful, motivating force in all of God's being. It deeply affects everything else God is and all that He does. One of our greatest needs as human beings is to be loved. We all need love. We need to know that we are important to somebody—that somebody truly cares about us, wants us, and accepts us unconditionally. God's love is extended to us even when we don't deserve it.

One of the calls of the prophetic voice is to reveal this nature of God to a love-deprived world. True prophetic voices must have their hearts tuned in to the heartbeat of God for the people we minister to. We must proclaim His love, seeing mankind as God sees them. Love is the humble concern for others more than yourself. Prophetic ministry is never about what you're looking at in the natural. It's always about what God has ordained from eternity. Prophets are the mouthpiece of God, and we must make sure we are saying what the Lord is saying with the right expression of His heart. We must speak to truth, which is sometimes corrective, in love.

> And I will raise up for Myself a faithful priest (Priest), who shall do according to what is in My heart and mind. And

> I will build him a sure house, and he shall walk before My
> anointed (Anointed) forever.
>
> —1 Samuel 2:35, amp

Notice in this passage of Scripture that the Lord states we must do all that is according to His heart and mind. It is not enough to have right words. We must also have the right expression and articulation. Sometimes the Lord reveals Himself as the Lion, the Lamb, or Judge, but the motivation is always love. Most people believe that Jesus is a judge wearing a black robe with a big gavel waiting to condemn them to hell. Daniel 7:9–10 shows a picture of the Ancient of Days who is the judge of mankind in a white robe and white hair. White robe and white hair symbolize the purity, holiness, and love the Lord has for mankind.

> If I speak in the tongues of men and of angels, but do not
> have love, I am a noisy gong or a clanging cymbal. And if
> I have prophecy, and know all mysteries and all knowledge,
> and if I have all faith so that I can remove mountains, but do
> not have love, I am nothing. If I give away everything I own,
> and if I give over my body in order to boast, but do not have
> love, I receive no benefit. Love is patient, love is kind, it is not
> envious. Love does not brag, it is not puffed up. It is not rude,
> it is not self-serving, it is not easily angered or resentful. It
> is not glad about injustice, but rejoices in the truth. It bears
> all things, believes all things, hopes all things, endures all
> things. Love never ends. But if there are prophecies, they will
> be set aside; if there are tongues, they will cease; if there is
> knowledge, it will be set aside. For we know in part, and we
> prophesy in part.
>
> —1 Corinthians 13:1–9, net

A prophet may possess all the charisma in the world, but if he or she does not have love, they are nothing. A prophet can prophesy with great accuracy and have all knowledge and great earth-shaking revelation but without love he or she is a like a noisy gong.

The speech is meaningless. Notice the passage says he is nothing without love. In other words ministering from a place of arrogance or superiority because of one's gift is seen as nothing in the eyes of God. We must always remember that if the Lord didn't gives us the gift or revelation or awaken us to our calling, we would be nothing. It is love that edifies and grows people into the stature of Christ, not mere knowledge. God's love is eternal, and nothing shall separate mankind from His unfailing love. Prophets are gifts given to the world motivated by love. They are to be the bridge that leads men back to the heart of God.

> Now about food offered to idols: of course we know that all of us possess knowledge [concerning these matters. Yet mere] knowledge causes people to be puffed up (to bear themselves loftily and be proud), but love (affection and goodwill and benevolence) edifies and builds up and encourages one to grow [to his full stature].
> —1 CORINTHIANS 8:1, AMP

> Eagerly pursue and seek to acquire [this] love [make it your aim, your great quest]; and earnestly desire and cultivate the spiritual endowments (gifts), especially that you may prophesy (interpret the divine will and purpose in inspired preaching and teaching).
> —1 CORINTHIANS 14:1, AMP

We must pursue love first, which will cause the desire for spiritual gifts to be pure. The banner of love protects the prophets and prophetic people from looking down on others or feeling more knowledgeable or equipped because of our prophetic gifting. Love is a safeguard against spiritual superiority or overblown sense of importance, because love does not brag or is puffed up. The more we pursue to love God and mankind, the greater the desire for spiritual gifts will be to minister and help win the world of men one soul at a time.

I was conducting a school of prophetic ministry in Europe where there were about two hundred people in attendance. I always close the school with an afternoon of personal prophecy for every attendee. I remember being extremely tired. I prayed to the Lord for grace and strength. The Holy Spirit prompted me to ask for Him to pour the love of God in my heart for the people. He said, "'Faith…worketh by love' (Gal. 5:6), and Romans 12:6 says that you prophesy according to the proportion of your faith and the gifts work by love, so I'm going to give you My supernatural love for all of these people, so you can have faith to prophesy to all two hundred of them."

What happened next was nothing short of miraculous. It was like a floodgate opened and out of my belly gushed rivers of living water. It was a true manifestation of John 7:38. Out of my innermost being prophetic ministry flowed continuously for about three hours—words of knowledge and words of wisdom laced with the compassion of Jesus. Love truly activates the gifts. I had a fresh revelation of what it means to move with compassion—compassion that loves the person but hates the bondage so much that you are moved to do something to free the victim from bondage. I believe the Lord will change the reputation of prophets where we've been known for our hard hearts and cold love. Prophets and prophetic people desire to be used of the Lord in this generation, but they must cultivate and make it their aim to truly pursue the love and compassion of Jesus for this incoming harvest of souls.

Here are some synonyms for *pursue*: camp on the doorstep of, give chase, go after, harass, harry, haunt, hound, hunt, hunt down, move behind, nose around, persevere, persist, plague, play catch up, poke around, prowl after, ride, run after, run down, scout out, search for, search high heaven, search out, seek, shadow, stalk, tag, tail, take out after, trace, track, track down, trail.

The Lord will equip an army of prophets and prophetic believers who will camp on the door of love. They will give chase to reveal the love of God to this generation. These prophetic soldiers will be armed with love-empowered prophetic words aimed at the hard-hearted, causing a generation to turn back to God.

The Call to Humility

Pride is the number one enemy of mankind. Pride separates man from dependence on God, but humility restores us to our position before God. (See Proverbs 18:12.)

> To the end that my glory may sing praise to thee, and not be silent. O LORD my God, I will give thanks unto thee forever.
>
> —PSALM 30:12

You tongue is your glory. Humility will cause you to yield your glory to His glory. The key to all ministry is found in nothingness and self-emptying in the presence of God. You will no longer compare yourself to others because you have given up every part of yourself in God's presence. Your posture is as one having nothing, seeking to be a servant of God.

God gives grace to the humble. The word is also called the word of His grace. The word ministers grace to the hearers.

> Now the man Moses was very meek, above all the men which were upon the face of the earth.
>
> —NUMBERS 12:3

Moses, one of the greatest prophets, was known for his meekness.

> The meek will he guide in judgment: and the meek will he teach his way.
>
> —PSALM 25:9

God guides the meek. The meek know the way of God. Prophets and prophetic people are concerned with the way of God. They desire more than the acts of God but desire His way. Those who are meek will have revelation of the way of God.

Take my yoke upon you, and learn of me; for I am meek and lowly in heart: and ye shall find rest unto your souls.

—MATTHEW 11:29

Meekness is the way of Christ. False prophets are arrogant and stubborn. False prophets do not manifest the character and humility of Christ. You cannot separate character from gifting. Character and gifting work together in prophets and prophetic people.

The Call to Purity

Blessed are the pure in heart: for they shall see God.

—MATTHEW 5:8

He that loveth pureness of heart, for the grace of his lips the king shall be his friend.

—PROVERBS 22:11

It is important to have a pure heart if you're going to see God or see with the eyes of God. The church is in desperate need of pure, authentic prophets and prophetic people who are upright in heart and demonstrate immaculate character and impeccable integrity. Prophets must learn how to conduct themselves in an exemplary manner because we are representatives of an excellent and majestic King.

Purity can be defined as the quality or state of being free from mixture, pollution, defilement, or other foreign elements. The term can refer to things or people. In the New Testament purity is used in an ethical and moral sense, meaning free from falsehood and without hidden motives.

The heart can be defined as the inner man—the function of mind, where man remembers and thinks. The heart is the seat and center of all physical and spiritual life. The soul or mind is the fountain and seat of thoughts, passions, desires, affections, appetites, purposes, and endeavors.[1]

In both passages of Scripture above we see the connection between purity of heart, sight, speech, and friendship with king.

"The king shall be his friend" is saying that the king will make him of his cabinet council. There was one in David's court and another in Solomon's. They were called the king's friend, or the man "in whose spirit there is no guile" (Ps. 32:2) and whose speech is always with grace. God will be his friend.

Prophets are coming who will be equipped with lips of grace and a supernatural ability to speak with fluency and persuasive power, using words appropriate to the circumstances. These prophets will represent the King's heart and be His confidant.

Purity in a prophet's life is spiritual at its root, and its fruits will reveal itself in humility and love. (See Matthew 5:8, James 1:27.) The religious leaders of Jesus's day always considered ceremonial purity more valuable than a heart for spiritual purity.

In 2 Peter 3:1 we find the Greek word *eilikrinēs*, which literally means "found pure when unfolded and examined by the sun's light."[2] The thought is that of judging something by the sunlight to expose any flaws. The only way the flaw of the heart is exposed is when it is held up to the light of the Son. Jeremiah 17:9 says, "The heart is deceitful above all things, and it is exceedingly perverse and corrupt and severely, mortally sick! Who can know it [perceive, understand, be acquainted with his own heart and mind]?" (AMP). The answer is only a visitation from the Lord can reveal what is truly in your heart. It takes an encounter with all-knowing God to reveal you to you.

The Process of Purity

> These people…honor Me with their lips but have removed their hearts far from Me.
>
> —ISAIAH 29:13, NKJV

Purity of heart, motives, and mind requires that prophets go through the processing of the Lord. It is not obtained overnight. It is requires time and death to self. John 12:24 says, "Unless a grain of wheat falls into the earth and dies, it remains alone; but if it dies, it bears much fruit" (RSV). I would like to take a look at Psalm 24 as David describes the place where purity is developed and glory is obtained.

The King of glory and His kingdom

> The earth is the LORD's, and all its fullness, the world and those who dwell therein. For He has founded it upon the seas, and established it upon the waters.
> —PSALM 24:1–2, NKJV

The truth is that all of the earth and all its people ultimately belong to the Lord. This is a reality that all prophets and prophetic believers must embrace. No one is untouchable when it comes to speaking the word of the Lord. It does not matter what race, nationality, and occupational position. God has a destiny, and we must extend our faith to minister.

Ascending to the hill of the Lord

> Who may ascend into the hill of the LORD? Or who may stand in His holy place?
> —PSALM 24:3, NKJV

Prophets must ascend to the hill of the Lord. The hill of the Lord is where we meet with God and our nature is changed. In the Bible hills and mountains were used interchangeably as sacred sites where prophets encountered God. Mount Horeb was where Moses encountered God at the burning bush. They were elevated places that made vision of an entire territory clear. It is the place where God shows you the light of His glory, and in the light of His glory you begin to see just how undone you are. This is the place where you get empowered for your ministry assignment. You are in an elevated place now and can see from the perspective of the Lord.

Ascend means to go up, to have a meeting, to retreat, to grow, to become a phenomenon when you come down, to extend the boundaries, to be superior, to stir up mentality to what you haven't seen before.

The divine question: Who?

Even though God loves all of His creation, there is a pattern for entering into His presence and walking in His delegated authority and power.

> He who has clean hands and a pure heart, who has not lifted up his soul to an idol, nor sworn deceitfully.
>
> —PSALM 24:4, NKJV

"Clean hands" represent those who walk and conduct their business with integrity. They possess inward holiness and practical ethics, demonstrating righteous actions.

"Pure heart" and motives are developed. Righteous thoughts and motives are the reasons for doing something, especially one that is hidden or not obvious.

"Who has not lifted his soul to an idol…" An idol can be anything you worship in the place of God. For example, your ministry reputation, job, and even children and accomplishments can all be idols. An idol is anything that you give devotion to over God.

The phrase "sworn deceitfully" speaks of telling lies or half-truths. A half-truth is a whole lie. Swearing deceitfully is when you intentionally speak a partial truth or a lie to benefit your self.

The face of God

> This is Jacob, the generation of those who seek Him, who seek
> Your face. Selah
>
> —PSALM 24:6, NKJV

> And Jacob was left alone; and there wrestled a man with him
> until the breaking of the day. And when he saw that he pre-
> vailed not against him, he touched the hollow of his thigh;
> and the hollow of Jacob's thigh was out of joint, as he wrestled
> with him. And he said, Let me go, for the day breaketh. And
> he said, I will not let thee go, except thou bless me. And he
> said unto him, What is thy name? And he said, Jacob. And
> he said, Thy name shall be called no more Jacob, but Israel:
> for as a prince hast thou power with God and with men, and
> hast prevailed. And Jacob asked him, and said, Tell me, I pray
> thee, thy name. And he said, Wherefore is it that thou dost ask
> after my name? And he blessed him there. And Jacob called
> the name of the place Peniel: for I have seen God face to face,
> and my life is preserved.
>
> —GENESIS 32:24–30

All through the Bible names have great significance. Names are
connected to the nature and character of a person. When God
changes the nature of someone, He also changes their name. Jacob
received Israel's prophecy. Many times when we're called into the
ministry, we have a nature just like Jacob's. But we must be sanc-
tified and purified to our call. We must meet the God of our call.
Jacob's name means he will supplant, he who supplants, he who
follows after, one who takes your heel, and one who a detainer. It
also means deceiver. Notice in the passage the man asked Jacob his
name. He had acknowledged his character flaw before he became
transformed.

Self-deception is a great enemy of the prophetic ministry. Because
prophets are called to lead mankind in the truth of the Lord, the
enemy will assign spirits of deception to their lives. It is imperative

that prophets experience personal transformation before they can bring transformation to their generation.

Peniel, a place mentioned in the verse above, is a place where one could behold the face of God. The name also means "facing God."[3]

The gates

> Lift up your heads, O you gates! And be lifted up, you everlasting doors! And the King of glory shall come in. Who is this King of glory? The Lord strong and mighty, the Lord mighty in battle. Lift up your heads, O you gates! Lift up, you everlasting doors! And the King of glory shall come in. Who is this King of glory? The Lord of hosts, He *is* the King of glory. Selah
>
> —Psalm 24:7–10, nkjv

The gate represents a place's entry and exit. Many times gates in Scripture are places where business is conducted. It is a place of authority. The Lord revealed to me that as prophets ascend to the hill of the Lord, they begin to gain authority to become the gate of glory.

The gate is not a geographical place. The prophet becomes the gateway of glory because the glory is in the human vessel. The glory can be defined as the manifested image of God. One of the major assignments of a prophet is to unlock the glory that's in earthen vessels or human beings.

The Lord has an agenda, and it's that the knowledge of His glory will cover the earth as the water covers the sea. When human beings are doing what they were created to do in the earth, they are manifesting the glory that God placed in them. Prophets are called to awaken many to the dimension of glory that has been placed in them from the almighty God.

Most Christians believe that if they stay in the church, fast, pray, and decree, a cloud of smoke will be released in the mayor's office and people will get saved and do the will of God. While fasting and praying are good, they are just the beginning phase. As saints on their jobs in the mayor's office work and look to be an example of the manifested image of God, which is the glory inside of them, then the knowledge of the glory of the Lord will cover the earth. As God ordained educators to devise programs that cause inner-city children's reading scores to improve or that songwriter to write songs about self-respect and purity, culture is changed. This is how the glory covers the earth. The majority of the body of Christ is not called to full-time pulpit ministry. They are called to the market-place where they will display the glory of the Lord to the world as they work in their God-ordained fields.

> But truly, as I live, all the earth shall be filled with the glory of the LORD.
>
> —NUMBERS 14:21, NKJV

The reason God calls a people to a place is to restore His glory. It is not simply to bless us, even though He will. It is always for a redemptive purpose. He has declared the earth shall be filled with His glory. *Glory* is honor, abundance, dignity, reputation, splendor, reverence, riches; a manifested image.

> For we are His workmanship, created in Christ Jesus for good works, which God prepared beforehand that we should walk in them.
>
> —EPHESIANS 2:10, NKJV

The Call to Holy Conversation

> But as he which hath called you is holy, so be ye holy in all manner of conversation;
>
> —1 PETER 1:15

Do not speak evil of one another, brethren. He who speaks evil of a brother and judges his brother, speaks evil of the law

and judges the law. But if you judge the law, you are not a doer
of the law but a judge.

—JAMES 4:11, NKJV

Evil speaking is also known by ancient rabbis as the "third tongue"[4]
because it destroys the speaker. It destroys the one spoken to, and
it destroys the one spoken about. It brings great defilement. The
Bible tells us it's not what goes into a man that defiles him but what
comes out.

Prophets should be especially careful about what they speak on
and to whom they speak. They represent God in everything they do.
When they initiate or participate in unholy conversation, they can
bring defilement on the listener and the person they are speaking
about. Sins of the mouth can hinder their prophetic flow.

Sins of the mouth that hinder prophetic flows

- Defilement—to pollute, to make unclean, to tarnish
  the purity of character by lewdness (Matt. 15:1–19;
  John 14:30)

- Lewdness—sinning in broad daylight with arrogance
  and contempt

- Idle words (Matt. 12:33–37)

- Backbiting—one who speaks against an absent individual (Ps. 15:1–3; Rom. 1:28–30)

- Busybody—one who seeks out information on a false
  report and spreads it by means of gossip, slander, and
  backbiting; a meddler in other people's affairs (1 Pet.
  4:15)

- Complaining—grumbling not loudly but so only those
  in close proximity can hear

- Slandering—trying to injure someone's reputation or character by sharing damaging stories about the past (Prov. 10:18)

- Talebearing (Lev. 19:16; Prov. 11:13; 17:9; 18:8; 26:20–22)

- Elaborating and exaggerating—making a story more dramatic

- Whispering—privately and secretly talking about other people; mumbling a spell (Prov. 16:28)

The Call to Servanthood

Surely the Lord GOD will do nothing, but he revealeth his secret unto his servants the prophets.

—AMOS 3:7

God has commissioned each prophet to fulfill a particular role, but every prophet is the servant of the Lord, and as servants they convey God's message to men. The Lord will give them special messages.

Prophets must understand that they are called to serve the body of Christ. They were not called so the body of Christ would serve them. The Lord will cause the "my ministry" spirit to die in prophets. Prophets must understand that the church is not a place to build their ministry and make a name for themselves. Prophets should always be concerned about the well-being and health of the church they are assigned to. Their goal should be to reveal truth from the heart of the Father that strengthens believers in the fulfillment of their destiny.

And they said, "Come, let us build ourselves a city, and a tower whose top is in the heavens; let us make a name for ourselves, lest we be scattered abroad over the face of the whole earth." But the LORD came down to see the city and the tower which the sons of men had built. And the LORD said, "Indeed the people are one and they all have one language, and this is what they begin to do; now nothing that they propose to do will be withheld from them. Come, let Us go down and there confuse their language, that they may not understand one another's speech." So the LORD scattered them abroad from there over the face of all the earth, and they ceased building the city. Therefore its name is called Babel, because there the LORD confused the language of all the earth; and from there the LORD scattered them abroad over the face of all the earth.

—GENESIS 11:4–9, NKJV

The tower of Babel demonstrated for us how confused language is birthed by selfish ambition, self-sufficiency, and making a name for oneself outside of dependency on God. When a prophet pollutes his or her call with selfish ambition and pride, their communication will be confused and his or her ministry scattered and shut down.

His scales are his pride, shut up together as with a close seal. One is so near to another, that no air can come between them. They are joined one to another, they stick together, that they cannot be sundered.

—JOB 41:15–17

He beholdeth all high things: he is a king over all the children of pride.

—JOB 41:34

Leviathan represents pride. His scales are his pride. His scales are so tight that no air can come between them. Air represents spirit. Pride will block the move of the spirit, including prophecy.

Humility is a key to operating in the prophetic and therefore should be a characteristic of prophetic people. Fasting is a way to humble the soul (Ps. 35:13). Fasting will bring about a level of humility. This is the opposite of pride (scales) that blocks the flow of the spirit. This humility will cause the prophet to be a rightful servant to the body of Christ and therefore fulfill the purpose that God commissioned him or her for in that season.

The prophetic is likened unto a flow. We don't want anything in our lives that would block the flow. Obstructions are like spiritual dams that stop, slow down, or impede the flow of a river.

> He that believeth on me, as the scripture hath said, out of his belly shall flow rivers of living water.
>
> —JOHN 7:38

> And they thirsted not when he led them through the deserts: he caused the waters to flow out of the rock for them: he clave the rock also, and the waters gushed out.
>
> —ISAIAH 48:21

In the verse just above we read that "the waters gushed out." In other words there was a strong flow. There was enough to satisfy those dwelling in the wilderness. Rivers of living water can flow from us. These rivers include prophetic rivers of edification, exhortation, and comfort.

The Cleansing of a Prophet

Those who have a prophetic calling on their lives should seek with all diligence to build up their character in the Lord. Love, humility, purity, holy conversation, and servanthood are key character attributes that prophets should be perfected in so that there is no hindrance to their flow. A holy character will enable a prophet to ascend into the holy hill of the Lord to receive His word for the people of God.

The Lord wants to cleanse and purify His prophets and prophetic believers so that they will be effective in turning this generation back to the heart of God. As I close this chapter, I want to look at how God purified Isaiah's heart, aligned his vision to His vision, and corrected his speech, causing Him to bow in humility and contrition. The Lord was then able to send him out on a new assignment. Prophets are called to make God known and to teach others about the knowledge of God. In order to do this well, prophets ought to be well acquainted with God themselves.

In Isaiah 6:1–4, we read:

> In the year that King Uzziah died, I saw the Lord sitting on a throne, high and lifted up, and the train of His robe filled the temple. Above it stood seraphim; each one had six wings: with two he covered his face, with two he covered his feet, and with two he flew. And one cried to another and said: "Holy, holy, holy is the Lord of hosts; the whole earth is full of His glory!" And the posts of the door were shaken by the voice of him who cried out, and the house was filled with smoke.
>
> —ISAIAH 6:1–4, NKJV

God's holiness is a part of everything He is and does. God's power is a *holy power.* God's love is a *holy love.* God's wisdom is a *holy wisdom.* Holiness is not an aspect of God's personality; it is one characteristic of His entire being. Prophets must exercise holiness because the call of God is holy. Holy apostles and prophets are being trained to represent a holy God.

The conviction of the prophet

Conviction is a major anointing that is needed in the prophetic ministry. The Scripture tells us that the gifts and the calling are without repentance. Many prophets operate in the gifts without having any conviction in their personal lives. *Conviction* can be defined as "the act of convincing a person of error or of compelling the admission of a truth."[5]

When you spend time in the presence of God, you are measured according to His standards, not the standards of man. In light of the Lord revealing Himself to Isaiah, he got a true picture of himself. Once Isaiah met with the Lord and was convicted of his sin and cleansed from his guilt, he was ready to serve God.

True conviction from the Holy Spirit releases an awareness that you've done something against the standard of the Lord, while on the other hand condemnation says *you* are something wrong.

> So I said: "Woe is me, for I am undone! Because I am a man of unclean lips, and I dwell in the midst of a people of unclean lips; for my eyes have seen the King, the LORD of hosts." Then one of the seraphim flew to me, having in his hand a live coal which he had taken with the tongs from the altar. And he touched my mouth with it, and said: "Behold, this has touched your lips; your iniquity is taken away, and your sin purged."
>
> —ISAIAH 6:5–7, NKJV

Isaiah's sin had to be *burned* away; the fire of judgment was applied to his place of sin. This was obviously a spiritual transaction. If one has a sinful mouth, it must be purged by the fire of God. It is an anointing from heaven.

Notice the Lord had to cleanse his lips, which represents speech. Isaiah saw his sinfulness and the sinfulness of his people, mainly in terms of sinful speech.

- By nature our lips are full of flattery and false intent: "With flattering lips and with a double heart do they speak" (Ps. 12:2).

- By nature lips lie and are proud: "Let the lying lips be put to silence; which speak grievous things proudly and contemptuously against the righteous" (Ps. 31:18).

- By nature lips deceive: "Keep your tongue from evil, and your lips from speaking deceit" (Ps. 34:13, NKJV).

- By nature lips are violent: "Swords are in their lips" (Ps. 59:7).

- By nature lips bring death to others: "The poison of asps is under their lips" (Ps. 140:3, NKJV).

Because of the Fall our carnal natures must be transformed before becoming the mouthpiece of God. The mouthpiece can be defined as a person who represents the views or opinions of another, a spokesperson who perpetuates the views or agenda of another. Purging of the tongue is purifying the speech.

Prophets can be very accurate, but this is not the litmus test for true prophetic ministry. It must be that they are walking in the nature of Christ. Prophets must mature to the full measure of the stature of Christ.

> Also I heard the voice of the Lord, saying: "Whom shall I send, and who will go for Us?" Then I said, "Here am I! Send me."
>
> —ISAIAH 6:8

Isaiah was a righteous, godly man by all outward appearance. Yet when he saw the enthroned King, the Lord of hosts, he saw how sinful he was in comparison. Authenticity comes from being with the Lord yourself. This is the hour when prophets must ascend the hill of the Lord and descend with truth and revelation from personal conviction. The Lord, not man, must give you your assignment. This process cuts away the strings and false allegiances in your life. Seeing the Lord for yourself will release a level of faith and courage to fulfill your assignment at all cost.

Prophets are sent from the presence of the Lord. The Lord imparts His vision, assignment, and heart to the prophet. Prophets must have a heart that has been processed in the presence of God. This will allow your heart to know its own sinfulness. Prophets develop a heart that knows the need among the people, the need for God's word. Prophets must have a heart that has been touched by God's cleansing fire.

Chapter 6

Roadblocks to Accuracy

*Woe to them! For they have gone in the way of
Cain, have run greedily in the error of Balaam for
profit, and perished in the rebellion of Korah.*

—JUDE 11, NKJV

CCURACY IS IMPORTANT to the prophet's ministry. *Accuracy* is defined as the quality or state of being correct or precise. There are things that can hinder and block accuracy, such as prejudices, misconceptions, doctrinal obsessions, sectarian views, bitterness, rejection, and lust. Prophets and prophetic people need to be careful that we guard our hearts against things that can block our prophetic flow and the accuracy of the word of the Lord.

> Can the fig tree, my brethren, bear olive berries? either a vine,
> figs? so can no fountain both yield salt water and fresh.
>
> —JAMES 3:12

Accuracy is important, and we want to speak what the Father gives us to speak. James talked about both sweet and bitter water coming from the same fountain. Our wells must be pure. What comes forth must be pure. Our fountains must be pure. We cannot allow ourselves to be hindered and bound by our own issues.

Here are some things that can be roadblocks to prophetic accuracy.

1. Too opinionated—Many prophetic people stumble because they feel that their opinion is God's opinion. God's thoughts are always higher than the thoughts of men. Many times prophets can become narrow-minded and dogmatic about revelations they believe to be a truth received from God.

2. Prejudices—This can be cultural or religious. This includes being prejudiced to a race, gender, age group, denomination, or movement.

3. Rejection and fear of rejection—Rejected people need deliverance or they will minister out of hurt. The priests could not have scabs (Lev. 21:20). Scabs are unhealed wounds that can become infected. Rejection leads to isolation, and prophets are called to associate and minister to people. Rejection can lead to prostituting the prophetic gift—prophets giving prophetic words to people just to be accepted by them. The root of this spirit is insecurity. Basically we reason with ourselves, saying, "I will get acceptance if I tell them what they want to hear." This also leads to flattery.

4. Fear of man—The Bible says, "The fear of man brings a snare" (Prov. 29:25, NKJV). "Snare" is the Greek *mowqesh*, which means to bait, lure. It's an iron ring placed in the nostril of a beast.[1] Fear of man leads us around like a beast with a ring in our nose. We must fear God more than man. The only way to overcome fear is to have faith in God.

5. Bitterness—Unresolved hurts lead to bitterness. Angry and bitter prophets can be tainted in their prophetic flow. Hebrews 12:15 says, "Looking carefully lest anyone fall short of the grace of God; lest any root of bitterness springing up cause trouble, and by this

many become defiled" (NKJV). Bitterness can be a root hidden in the heart going undetected. This heart condition springs up at the most inopportune time.

6. Respect of persons—This can be a religious spirit. The high priest carried the stones of all the tribes on his heart, and we should carry the whole church in our hearts and not be limited to organizations and denominations. True prophetic ministry will learn how to minister the word of the Lord to all kinds of people and denominations because Jesus is Lord of all the earth. God likes variety and different tribes; that is why He had twelve of them. A Baptist preacher once told me, "I'm Baptist born and Baptist bred, and when I die I'll be Baptist dead." Some people will never leave the church denomination, and this shouldn't disqualify them from receiving a prophetic word. The prophetic anointing is not designed to change church culture; it's designed to change the hearts and minds of the people who affect the culture. God loves the Baptists. He even had one in the New Testament—John the Baptist. Prophecy is never used to establish new principles in a denomination or organization. A skilled prophetic minister can deliver the heart of God without partiality. I found that many different denomination leaders have invited me to teach and train their people in the prophetic because of trust and relationship. James 2:9 says, "But if ye have respect to persons, ye commit sin, and are convinced of the law as transgressors."

7. Human compassion—This is having compassion on that which God is judging. Jesus rebuked Peter and said, "Get thee behind me, Satan" (Matt. 16:23). Jesus spoke what He saw the Father doing. Prophets cannot

allow human compassion to dictate their prophetic flow. There are times you need to minister correction to people you love, and it can be hard, but prophets must pledge their allegiance to the Lamb of God. Prophesying truth brings deliverance to the hearer. I have learned that every time I neglect to speak the truth to someone, I lose my power to discern or my hearing in that situation becomes dull.

8. Judgmental—This is the opposite of mercy, and when one has a religious spirit he can point out problems with great accuracy but seldom have a solution. All they have done is judged and torn down. Beware of pride and being overcritical. The critical prophet with pointing of the finger is not ministering out of the heart of God.

9. Judging by appearance—Looking at a person's hand for a ring before giving a word about marriage or looking at someone's countenance for some emotional signals is judging by appearance. Samuel had to anoint David although he was a boy. God told the prophet to judge not according to appearance (1 Sam. 16:7).

10. Lust—The simple definition of *lust* is having a self-absorbed desire for an object, person, or experience. When we are in lust, we place the object of our desire above all. Prophets must guard their hearts from the lust for power, prestige, promotion, and wealth. Lust in these areas will cause you to be drawn away from the will of God into a place of error and deception. Unresolved lust issues of the heart have serious implications to the validity of a prophet's ministry. These lust issues create stumbling blocks to accurate prophetic ministry. If you're not delivered from

them, they can entice and drag you down a path of falsehood, causing you to potentially become a false prophet. "But every man is tempted, when he is drawn away of his own lust, and enticed" (James 1:14).

Being developed in a sectarian environment is not the best for a prophet. It can warrant any of these issues to taint or color the way a prophet delivers the word of the Lord. Prophets have to be developed in the proper environment, else they can develop or be influenced by religious spirits. Religious spirits are real, and they can work in the environment of churches and sectarian groups. Religious spirits work where people believe in prophecy and the gifts of the Spirit. We need discernment and deliverance to avoid contamination.

Prophets cannot allow any bias to affect their words. Bias is prejudice in favor of or against one thing, person, or group compared with another, usually in a way considered to be unfair. God is fair, and He is no respecter of persons.

How to Come Against Roadblocks

A roadblock is a barricade or obstruction across a road set up to prevent the escape or passage. The above-mentioned roadblocks have the potential detour us from the God-ordained path for our lives. Sometimes they can be hidden issues of the heart that only the Holy Spirit can reveal. Prophets and prophetic people must develop the discipline of self-examination. Psalm 51 is one of my favorite psalms. Praying it over my life has been a major tool to developing self-examination. David prayed in Psalm 51:6 that God desires truth in the inward parts and in the hidden part He shall make us to know wisdom.

Step 1: Desire truth in your inward parts.

The first step to overcoming these stumbling blocks is having a desire for truth in the inward parts. We should desire truth that is not superficial, but truth that reaches far deeper than a mere intellectual comprehension of truth; it is truth that reaches down into the depth our being. The opposite of the truth is deception. The worst kind of deception is self-deception. The power of deception is the person being deceived believes that he is being led of the Lord. It takes the mercy and power of the Holy Spirit to break through deception.

Step 2: Allow the Holy Spirit to search your heart.

The second step to overcoming roadblocks is to allow the Holy Spirit to search your heart, shining a light on any wicked area. The Holy Spirit is the Spirit of truth. He will give you wisdom in the hidden areas of heart. Psalm 139:23 says, "Search me [thoroughly], O God, and know my heart! Try me and know my thoughts! And see if there is any wicked or hurtful way in me, and lead me in the way everlasting" (AMP). Once the Holy Spirit searches your heart and reveals blocks and flaws, you must be honest with yourself and not try to justify your actions. David states in Psalm 51:3 that he acknowledged his sin and transgression. Recognizing sin and error requires humility and brokenness. It's also the first step to healing and deliverance.

Step 3: Repent immediately.

The third step to overcoming roadblocks is to immediately repent. Once the Holy Spirit convicts you of a roadblock, there is an anointing in that moment to be healed, delivered, and transformed. Delayed response can lead to hardness of heart and greater deception. *Repent* comes from the Greek word *metanoia*. In this compound word the preposition combines the two meanings of "time" and "change," which may be denoted by "after" and "different"; so that the whole compound means: "to think differently after," "a change of mind accompanied by regret and change of conduct," "a change of mind and heart," or "a change of consciousness."[2] Based on this definition, repentance means, after the Holy Spirit has revealed information, you change your way of thinking. The wrong road will never become the right road. The only way to get on the right road is to discover where you made a detour and turn around immediately.

Step 4: Rend your heart.

The fourth step to overcoming roadblocks is to rend the heart. In Joel's day people tore their garments to show their grief and desperation. However, what God desires is the tearing of our hearts, which speaks of dealing radically with the matters of our heart.

To rend means to tear something violently or forcibly. We tear our heart away from everything in our lives that quenches or blocks the pure flow of the Spirit! Tearing our heart is intensely personal and painful. Some want the Spirit to free them from their sinful patterns without it requiring any personal choices that tear their heart. That is not the way it happens.

> And rend your heart, and not your garments, and turn unto the LORD your God: for he is gracious and merciful, slow to anger, and of great kindness, and repenteth him of the evil.
>
> —JOEL 2:13

The Progression of a False Prophet

Accuracy in prophetic ministry is important and should be pursued and cultivated in a prophet's and prophetic minister's life, but it is not the litmus test of a true prophet. I would look at the life of Balaam who was an accurate prophesier but a false prophet.

> Woe to them! For they have gone in the way of Cain, have run
> greedily in the error of Balaam for profit, and perished in the
> rebellion of Korah.
>
> —Jude 11, NKJV

Balaam is a perfect example of a prophet who didn't take the steps to overcome the roadblocks of lust, respect of persons, and self-will. Balaam had a lust for power, prestige, money, and honor that enticed him down a road of falsehood. These demonic assignments found common ground in his heart. *Entice* means to draw on by exciting hope or desire; to allure; to attract; as, the bait enticed the fishes. Often in a bad sense it means to lead astray; to induce to evil; to tempt; as, the sirens enticed them to listen. Balaam's lust and self-will led down a road of destruction that caused him to die as soothsayer (Josh. 13:22). Death is also the end result of lust and self-will. (See James 1:12–15).

Let's take a close look in Scripture in Numbers 22 at the life of Balaam. There are many character flaws that must be avoided.

Balaam had an accurate gift that got the attention of King Balak. He developed a reputation for making predictions that were fulfilled. His fame reached Balak hundreds of miles away. He was known for accurately prophesying and pronouncing a blessing or curse on people. There was something in the way that Balaam administered his prophetic gift that indicated to King Balak that he could be bought. His methods of ministry didn't distinguish him as a prophet of the Lord.

Here's a lesson for prophetic people: we must be in the world but not of the world. There must be clear lines of demarcation regarding the source of our prophetic ministry. Our prophetic ministry should not mimic the world. First Samuel 3:20 states that Samuel was established as prophet in all of Israel. Elijah fearlessly and boldly announced to King Ahab that he stood in obedient service to the God of Israel. (See 1 Kings 17:1.)

There is a requirement to being a prophet of the Lord, and it is holiness. *Holiness* means to be separated and consecrated to the Lord.

The elders enticed Balaam with reward of foretelling or, as the King James Version states, "the rewards of divination" (Num. 22:7). The rewards of divination were commonly know as money that procures divination or as interpreted in 2 Peter 2:15 "the wages of unrighteousness." When a true prophet develops a reputation for accurately ministering words from the Lord, temptation can arise to sell the gift for money. I call this prostituting the gift.

In Numbers 22:8 we find a perfect example of knowing the actions of God but not the ways of God. (See Psalms 103:7.) Balaam knew how to demonstrate and operate in the acts of God. But Balaam did not have an intimate knowledge of God Himself.

Prophets can't live out of their gift. They must spend time in the presence of the Lord learning His ways. God loves His covenant people. Balaam should have known that it was the power of Lord that caused the children of Israel to destroy the Amorites, multiply, and possess the land. God was the very source of King Balak's fear (Num. 21:33–35).

In Numbers 22:9–12 the Lord asked Balaam a question. Do you really think that the God who knows everything did not already know the answer to His question? God wasn't looking for an answer. He was measuring the motives of Balaam's heart. This was the question that should have provoked self-examination. Prophets must understand that when the omniscient God asks you a question, it's your responsibility to find out the answer.

In verse 19 we see the heart of the matter of Balaam's idolatry. By agreeing to inquire again of Jehovah after already knowing the will of God, he revealed a secret desire for the reward of divination. Balaam's lust for promotion, influence, and wealth enticed him to inquire of the God of Israel instead of cutting off the negotiation.

Prophets must guard their hearts from idolatry. Idolatry in the heart perverts our hearing purely from the Lord. Instead of living for God, we began to live for ourselves, our ministry, our reputation, or for material goods.

Prophets should be sure and certain that promotion doesn't come from the east or the west; promotion doesn't come from anyone on earth. It comes from God above (Ps. 75:6–7). You cannot connive and manipulate your way into a promotion. You must humble yourself under the mighty hand of God, and He will exalt you in due season. Self-promotion leads to false ministry. One of the judgments of God is to have success in the wrong area.

The million-dollar question is why did God give Balaam permission to go and then appear to be angered by his actions (Num. 22:20–22)? The answer is found in how God deals with idols of the heart. God will answer according to multitudes of idols in your heart. (See Ezekiel 14:1–5.) What the heart has chosen the Lord allows. The Lord will never override the human will. The Lord revealed His will, but Balaam chose to not completely follow the will of the Lord. Instead he allowed the idol of self-will to take root in his heart, which led him to a place of disobedience.

The calling of a prophet is not about operating in an accurate gift. It is about the total man representing the will of the Lord. Prophets must become the message to their generation. We cannot allow idols in our hearts to cause us to be estranged from the divine will of the Lord.

Prophets must learn to die to self and cause their self-will to align with the will of the Lord. The idol of self-will causes you to stumble in fulfilling your destiny. The life of Christ gives some keys to death to self-will (Matt 26:36–41).

- First you must go to Garden of Gethsemane. *Gethsemane* means the oil press. This is place where you allow God to purge of all your agendas, opinions, and idols out your heart.

- Second you must realize that you can be tempted to go another way than the revealed will of the Lord. Jesus asked the Father if there was another way than the cross. He proclaimed, "Nevertheless not as I will, but as thou wilt" (v. 39). He died to self so that multitudes my live. This is the call of the prophet: to die to self that others may live.

- Finally you must watch and pray so that you don't come into temptation. This is developing a life of devotion to the Lord, keeping your heart on the altar of God as a lifestyle.

It is amazing that Balaam believed in such supernatural events as an animal that can talk and reason (Num. 22:24–30), but he was blind to the fact that he was opposing the Lord. Prophets must understand that just because they are having dreams, visions, and supernatural encounters does not mean they're in the perfect will of the Lord. I am convinced supernatural encounters alone are not enough to bring transformation to the heart. We must choose life or death. We must choose the will of the Lord.

Balaam was selfish. King Balak wanted to destroy the people of God. He was only concerned for his promotion and financial gain. Balaam's name means devourer of the people. Jude 12 states that he was feeding himself without fear. True prophets will service people, but false people devour the people.

Chapter 7

The Voice of the Lord

And they heard the voice of the Lord God walking in the garden
in the cool of the day: and Adam and his wife hid themselves from
the presence of the Lord God amongst the trees of the garden.

—Genesis 3:8

THE BOOK OF Genesis records the first mention of the voice of the Lord. Adam and Eve hid from God's presence when they heard His voice. Notice that the voice of the Lord is connected to the presence of the Lord. Whenever God's presence is strong, we can expect to hear His voice.

This is an hour when God wants His people to draw near to Him and not hide from His voice. The Fall caused Adam and Eve to be ashamed and hide from the voice of God. Sin separated man from God, meaning he could no longer hear and perceive the motives and intentions of the heart of God. Many have the wrong perspective as it relates to God. Jesus came to restore our relationship with God the Father. He wants His children to hear and know His voice. God desires to fellowship and have relationship with His creation. God inspires prophets and prophetic people to release His voice to His children. Prophets should communicate, articulate, and give voice to the heart of God. True prophetic messages should send you into the presence of the Father.

> The voice of the Lord is powerful; the voice of the Lord is full of majesty.
>
> —Psalm 29:4

There is a power released that shakes the heaven and shifts things on earth. When prophets release words from the King of glory, change happens on the earth. The voice of the Lord is full of majesty. God doesn't want to just release information about Himself; He also wants to release the essence of who He is. Majesty is defined as supreme greatness or authority. When prophets prophesy, they release an awareness of the supreme greatness of God. Many times when prophets prophesy, they release the spirit of the fear of the Lord.

> The voice of the Lord breaketh the cedars; yea, the Lord breaketh the cedars of Lebanon.
>
> —Psalm 29:5

The cedars of Lebanon are mighty trees of God, which under normal circumstances have the strength to withstand the forces of nature. One commentary says that the voice of the Lord splinters the tree into matchsticks (Ps. 29:5–6).[1] Many times in Scripture trees are symbolic of men. The voice of the Lord breaks yokes. One word from the voice of the Lord can bring brokenness and humility. Prophecy is a powerful tool to deal with stiff-necked pride and hardness of heart.

> The voice of the Lord divideth the flames of fire.
>
> —Psalm 29:7

The voice of the Lord through the mouth of prophets sends out flames of fire, bringing revival to the heart. There is a power released to penetrate, melt, enlighten, and inflame the hearts of men.

> The voice of the Lord shaketh the wilderness; the Lord shaketh the wilderness of Kadesh.
>
> —Psalm 29:8

The voice of the Lord shakes or unsettles things in our lives. It brings impact and rearrangement in our lives.

> The voice of the LORD maketh the hinds to calve, and discovereth the forests: and in his temple doth every one speak of his glory.
> —PSALM 29:9

The voice of the Lord activates and births new things in the church. It also brings exposure and insight.

> For through the voice of the LORD shall the Assyrian be beaten down, which smote with a rod.
> —ISAIAH 30:31

The Lord is releasing prophets with words in their mouths that shall beat down the powers of darkness. The Lord is a breaker, and He is releasing an anointing to break every yoke that has been placed on His children.

> When he uttereth his voice, there is a multitude of waters in the heavens, and he causeth the vapours to ascend from the ends of the earth; he maketh lightnings with rain, and bringeth forth the wind out of his treasures.
> —JEREMIAH 10:13

> And the LORD shall utter his voice before his army: for his camp is very great: for he is strong that executeth his word: for the day of the LORD is great and very terrible; and who can abide it?
> —JOEL 2:11

These scriptures give us a revelation of the power of the voice of the Lord. When God speaks, things happen. When God speaks through us, things happen. We can never underestimate the power of God's voice.

This is why prophecy is so important. Prophecy is the voice of the Lord through us. God utters His voice and executes His word. In other words He carries out what He speaks.

The Holy Spirit and Prophecy

> And it shall come to pass in the last days, saith God, I will pour out of my Spirit upon all flesh: and your sons and your daughters shall prophesy, and your young men shall see visions, and your old men shall dream dreams: and on my servants and on my handmaidens I will pour out in those days of my Spirit; and they shall prophesy.
>
> —ACTS 2:17–18; see also Joel 2:28–29

The Holy Spirit is the doorway to the prophetic realm. All flesh can partake of this and enter through this door. This is God's abundant nature.

> Restore unto me the joy of thy salvation; and uphold me with thy free spirit.
>
> —PSALM 51:12

The Holy Spirit is called a free Spirit. *Free* is the Hebrew word *nadiyb*, meaning generous, willing, and spontaneous.[2] God is willing and generous to speak to us and through us.

The new covenant opens the way for all of God's people to partake of this to some degree. All are not prophets, but all can prophesy to some degree. The Day of Pentecost was a marker for a new day in prophecy, with the result being the sons, daughters, servants, handmaidens, young men, and old men all having access to the prophetic realm.

This is good news. The good news of the kingdom has arrived. The good news of salvation has come. The gospel brought a release of the Holy Spirit and the prophetic.

> And Moses said unto him, Enviest thou for my sake? would
> God that all the LORD's people were prophets, and that the
> LORD would put his spirit upon them!
> —NUMBERS 11:29

This heart and cry of Moses was that the Holy Spirit would come upon all. The seventy elders who partook of Moses's spirit began to prophesy. We now partake of Christ's Spirit, and we prophesy. What a glorious blessing and privilege.

We need not be envious of anyone who prophesies because we can all prophesy. There need not be any competition in this area. The outpouring of the Spirit breaks gender barriers (sons and daughter), social barriers (servants and handmaidens), and age barriers (young and old).

> But this shall be the covenant that I will make with the house
> of Israel; after those days, saith the LORD, I will put my law in
> their inward parts, and write it in their hearts; and will be their
> God, and they shall be my people. And they shall teach no more
> every man his neighbour, and every man his brother, saying,
> Know the LORD: for they shall all know me, from the least of
> them unto the greatest of them, saith the LORD: for I will for-
> give their iniquity, and I will remember their sin no more.
> —JEREMIAH 31:33–34

All can know God, from the least to the greatest, under this new covenant. All can partake of the Holy Spirit. All can enter into the prophetic realm. All can hear and know the voice of God. Although there are different gifts and abilities, the new covenant is a great equalizer.

All Are Not Prophets

> Are all apostles? are all prophets? are all teachers? are all
> workers of miracles?
> —1 CORINTHIANS 12:29

I am not implying that all are prophets. I am saying that all can enter into the prophetic realm through the Holy Spirit. There is a gift of prophecy, and there is an office of the prophet. These are special gifts and assignments given to some for God's purposes.

Each gift has its proper place and function. There is also the gift of the Holy Spirit. All of God's people can receive this gift, and the result will be utterance.

> And they were all filled with the Holy Ghost, and began to speak with other tongues, as the Spirit gave them utterance.
>
> —ACTS 2:4

The Holy Spirit gave them utterance. Prophecy is utterance. Prophets will have utterance. Those with the gift of prophecy will have utterance. The strength and power of these utterances will be based on the gifting. All of God's people can have utterance. As a matter of fact we should be enriched in utterance.

> That in every thing ye are enriched by him, in all utterance, and in all knowledge.
>
> —1 CORINTHIANS 1:5

Enriched means to make rich or richer especially by the addition or increase of some desirable quality, attribute, or ingredient. We should also abound in utterance.

> Therefore, as ye abound in every thing, in faith, and utterance, and knowledge, and in all diligence, and in your love to us, see that ye abound in this grace also.
>
> —2 CORINTHIANS 8:7

The outpouring of the Holy Spirit resulted in an abundance of utterance. We are told not to stifle the utterances of the Holy Spirit.

Do not spurn the gifts and utterances of the prophets [do not depreciate prophetic revelations nor despise inspired instruction or exhortation or warning].

—1 Thessalonians 5:20, AMP

Utterance is important because it is the mode of communication. God communicates with His people through utterance. We communicate with God through utterance. The Day of Pentecost saw the fulfillment of Joel's prophecy with the release of a new level of utterance.

There is a time and place selected by God to release these utterances. These utterances are released to fulfill the purpose of God. People respond to utterance. They can either accept it or reject it.

Prophets and prophetic people are anointed by the Holy Spirit to release these utterances. There are a great variety of delivery styles. There are different administrations and operations of the Spirit, but utterance is an important aspect of the prophetic. Without utterance the prophetic cannot operate or be released.

As I mentioned previously, the right word at the right time carries tremendous power. (See Job 6:25.) God has a word at the right time for every situation. I call this a word in season.

The Lord God hath given me the tongue of the learned, that I should know how to speak a word in season to him that is weary: he wakeneth morning by morning, he wakeneth mine ear to hear as the learned.

—Isaiah 50:4

There is a right word in season for the weary. This is the tongue of the learned. Those who are learned in the prophetic can speak this word. Those who are learned in the ways of the Holy Spirit can speak this word. Those who have been instructed by God can speak this word. Our ears can be awakened to hear this word, and our tongues can be instructed to speak it.

Chapter 8

Prophetic Diversity

And there are differences of administrations, but the
same LORD. And there are diversities of operations,
but it is the same God which worketh all in all.

—1 CORINTHIANS 12:5–6

LTHOUGH ALL CAN enter the prophetic realm through the
Holy Spirit, there is great diversity within this realm. Even
creation reveals that our God is a God of diversity. We
must not try to make all prophetic people the same, although they
may have some similarities.

Elijah is often used as a picture of the prophet. Samuel was a
priest and a prophet. Moses was a prophet who was also a lawgiver.
David was a king and a prophet. David was also a musical prophet.
There were other musical prophets such as Heman, Asaph, and
Jeduthun. Daniel was a prophet who was also a government official.
John was a prophet who did no miracles, and Elisha did twice as
many miracles as Elijah.

Anna was a prophetess who prayed and fasted day and night.
Deborah was a prophetess and a judge. Jeremiah was a weeping
prophet who mourned over the sins of Israel. Barnabas was an
encouraging prophet (his name means son of consolation). Jesus is
the prophet spoken of by Moses.

There is also the gift of prophecy that is a manifestation of the

Holy Spirit (1 Cor. 12:10). This gift can manifest through believers, apostles, prophets, evangelists, pastors, and teachers.

There is the spirit of prophecy that usually comes with worship. The spirit of prophecy is the testimony of Jesus. Jesus can speak through anyone, especially when the presence of His Spirit is strong and especially as a result of worship (Rev. 19:10).

People can also prophesy as a result of being filled with the Holy Ghost (Acts 19:6). The Holy Spirit can give any believer inspired utterance. The Holy Spirit is the doorway into the prophetic.

There are different levels of the prophetic. The prophet has a mantle that carries a tremendous amount of power and authority. The prophet carries an extraordinary grace to break through, and the utterances of a prophet can root out, tear down, throw down, destroy, build, and plant (Jer. 1:10). As previously stated, there are diversities among prophets.

Prophets encourage God's people to trust in God alone and not to bow before human strength. They firmly believe that God is the almighty ruler of the universe, the moral governor of the world. They impart relentless faith in the true and living God and that He alone controls all things. God's people should obey Him and not the empty threats of man.

The major message of the prophet is the Lordship of Jesus Christ. They urge men to know, believe, and practice the Word of God. The Lord reveals the sinfulness and perversity of man, requiring the prophet to preach repentance and returning obediently to God. They preach conversion and salvation. Many believers are saved to go to heaven but not converted to advance the kingdom.

The prophet's anointing can be expressed in a variety of ways.

Prophets can operate in teaching, preaching, singing, dancing, praying, counseling, building, planting, establishing, imparting, encouraging, confirming, correcting, comforting, strengthening, evangelizing, healing, delivering, and miracles.

Prophets who have a strong teaching gift are usually used as prophetic equippers. They help make disciples and fulfill the mandate of bringing unity, intimacy, and maturity to the body of Christ. These are Samuel-type prophets who establish and plant schools to reproduce sons and daughters to carry the prophetic mantles. They are interested in seeing the prophetic anointing increased and multiplied with accuracy from generation to generation. It takes mature prophets to train emerging prophets. We must not let a cycle of deterioration occur in the prophetic movement. The prophetic should not be occasional in the church.

Prophetic Impartation

Prophets are also important in imparting a prophetic spirit to the church. A church cannot be prophetic without prophets. Prophets need to be an active part of the church and are instrumental in releasing others into the prophetic realm.

"Impart" is the Greek word *metadidōmi*, meaning to share a thing with anyone.[1] It means to give, convey, or grant from or as if from a store. Impartation is not limited to prophets, but prophets have a great ability to impart into the lives of those they minister to. Prophets are spiritual people, and impartation is a spiritual dynamic. Prophets and prophecy are vehicles through which God imparts great blessing to the believers.

Some churches and ministries are known for releasing many strong ministries. This is usually due to the power of impartation. An atmosphere of prayer, worship, fasting, and prophecy is conducive for impartation.

An example of this is Ramah. Many prophets were developed and trained in Ramah by Samuel. A major part of this was impartation.

> And Saul sent messengers to take David: and when they saw the company of the prophets prophesying, and Samuel standing as appointed over them, the Spirit of God was upon the messengers of Saul, and they also prophesied. And when it was told Saul, he sent other messengers, and they prophesied

likewise. And Saul sent messengers again the third time, and they prophesied also.

—1 SAMUEL 19:20–21

We see impartation in the ministry of Moses.

And Joshua the son of Nun was full of the spirit of wisdom; for Moses had laid his hands upon him: and the children of Israel hearkened unto him, and did as the LORD commanded Moses.

—DEUTERONOMY 34:9

Moses imparted the spirit of wisdom into Joshua through the laying on of hands. Prophets are used by God to impart gifts into people.

For I long to see you, that I may impart unto you some spiritual gift, to the end ye may be established.

—ROMANS 1:11

Paul desired to impart spiritual gifts to the Romans so they could be established. Ministry gifts, including prophets, should have a desire to impart. Prophets are not selfish. Prophets desire to see others trained and raised up. Impartation releases strength to the church and individual believers.

Neglect not the gift that is in thee, which was given thee by prophecy, with the laying on of the hands of the presbytery.

—1 TIMOTHY 4:14

Timothy received a spiritual gift through prophecy with the laying on of hands of the elders. Prophets have an ability to impart. Impartation results in the manifestation of spiritual gifts in the assembly.

> Wherefore I put thee in remembrance that thou stir up the
> gift of God, which is in thee by the putting on of my hands.
>
> —2 TIMOTHY 1:6

Believers can receive spiritual gifts directly from God through the Holy Spirit. The Holy Spirit also uses individuals to impart gifts into our lives. Timothy received a gift through the laying on of hands of the apostle. Jesus imparted power and authority to the disciples.

> And when he had called unto him his twelve disciples, he gave
> them power against unclean spirits, to cast them out, and to
> heal all manner of sickness and all manner of disease.
>
> —MATTHEW 10:1

Elijah cast his mantle upon Elisha. The mantle was a symbol of the anointing.

> So Elijah left there and found Elisha son of Shaphat, whose
> plowing was being done with twelve yoke of oxen, and he
> drove the twelfth. Elijah crossed over to him and cast his
> mantle upon him. He left the oxen and ran after Elijah and
> said, Let me kiss my father and mother, and then I will follow
> you. And he [testing Elisha] said, Go on back. What have I
> done to you? [Settle it for yourself.] So Elisha went back from
> him. Then he took a yoke of oxen, slew them, boiled their flesh
> with the oxen's yoke [as fuel], and gave to the people, and they
> ate. Then he arose, followed Elijah, and served him.
>
> —1 KINGS 19:19–21, AMP

Notice in this passage Elisha was demonstrating a work ethic. He was already demonstrating a sense of responsibility in his father's field. This positioned him for promotion and impartation. Elisha had a double portion and twice the miracles of Elijah, which means he did twice the work.

Many Christians never progress into higher levels of anointing because they never use the impartation properly. Impartations are not just to make you more spiritual. They are for the work of the ministry. Once the mantle or impartation is given, your response determines the level of fulfillment.

Elisha also honored his parents and those he was connected to by celebration. We must celebrate and honor those who have imparted in our lives as we transition to new seasons of ministry.

Elisha later received a double portion of Elijah's spirit. His anointing brought restoration in the personal lives through miracles. He ministered to people and their problems. Impartations are to help people in their destinies.

> As they still went on and talked, behold, a chariot of fire and horses of fire parted the two of them, and Elijah went up by a whirlwind into heaven. And Elisha saw it and he cried, My father, my father! The chariot of Israel and its horsemen! And he saw him no more. And he took hold of his own clothes and tore them in two pieces. He took up also the mantle of Elijah that fell from him and went back and stood by the bank of the Jordan. And he took the mantle that fell from Elijah and struck the waters and said, Where is the Lord, the God of Elijah? And when he had struck the waters, they parted this way and that, and Elisha went over.
>
> —2 KINGS 2:11–14, AMP

Elisha tore his garment in two pieces before he could put on the new mantle and walk in the double portion of Elijah's mantle. This represents leaving the old familiar season to walking into the new season. You must leave something to enter into something new. The mantle symbolized an impartation of authority and power given by God. He took the mantle and struck the waters. He wouldn't have ever known if the impartation was there if he didn't use it. True authority isn't authority until you use it.

> And when the sons of the prophets which were to view at Jericho saw him, they said, The spirit of Elijah doth rest on Elisha. And they came to meet him, and bowed themselves to the ground before him.
>
> —2 KINGS 2:15

This shows that mantles and anointings can be imparted and transferred. God took the spirit that was upon Moses and placed it upon the seventy elders of Israel, and they prophesied.

> And the LORD came down in a cloud, and spake unto him, and took of the spirit that was upon him, and gave it unto the seventy elders: and it came to pass, that, when the spirit rested upon them, they prophesied, and did not cease.
>
> —NUMBERS 11:25

Saul began to prophesy when he came into contact with the company of prophets.

> After that thou shalt come to the hill of God, where is the garrison of the Philistines: and it shall come to pass, when thou art come thither to the city, that thou shalt meet a company of prophets coming down from the high place with a psaltery, and a tabret, and a pipe, and a harp, before them; and they shall prophesy: And the Spirit of the LORD will come upon thee, and thou shalt prophesy with them, and shalt be turned into another man.
>
> —1 SAMUEL 10:5–6

> And when they came thither to the hill, behold, a company of prophets met him; and the Spirit of God came upon him, and he prophesied among them.
>
> —1 SAMUEL 10:10

Saul was turned into another man by coming into contact with a company of prophets. He was changed and elevated to a higher spiritual realm. This is the power of impartation.

These are all biblical examples of impartation. Prophets and other ministry gifts are channels through which blessings flow. Impartation can come through preaching, teaching, prophecy, laying on of hands, and association.

Impartation is not done haphazardly or indiscriminately. Simon the sorcerer was rebuked for desiring the ability to release the Holy Spirit.

> Then laid they their hands on them, and they received the Holy Ghost. And when Simon saw that through laying on of the apostles' hands the Holy Ghost was given, he offered them money, saying, Give me also this power, that on whomsoever I lay hands, he may receive the Holy Ghost.
>
> —ACTS 8:17–19

Impartation cannot be bought with money. It is a spiritual transfer from spiritually qualified people. Churches and individuals will receive a greater measure of anointing and gifting through impartation. Leaders would be wise to have qualified prophets minister to the church in order to see the people elevated into greater grace and ability.

> Let the prophets speak two or three, and let the other judge.
>
> —1 CORINTHIANS 14:29

Prophets can and should minister in teams and companies. Prophetic teams in local churches can be a great blessing to the church. Prophets stir one another, and they provide balance and accountability to one another.

Chapter 9

Different Kinds of Prophetic Words

For God speaketh once, yea twice, yet man perceiveth it not.

—JOB 33:14

HERE ARE DIFFERENT kinds of prophetic words for different situations. The prophetic word can deal with past, present, and future. The prophetic word is able to deal with all the issues that we face in life. God has many thoughts toward us, and if we were to speak them, they cannot be numbered (Ps. 40:5). God's word is a lamp unto our feet and a light unto our path (Ps. 119:105). Sometimes these different aspects can flow together in one prophecy.

Here are the various kinds of words that can be delivered through prophecy.

1. A word in season—addresses issues that are currently happening in a person's life. This prophetic word gives understanding into what a person is dealing with and helps eliminate confusion (Isa. 50:4).

The Lord GOD has given Me the tongue of the learned, that I should know how to speak a word in season to him who is weary. He awakens Me morning by morning, He awakens My ear to hear as the learned.

—ISAIAH 50:4, NKJV

While in South Africa some time before Mother's Day I was awakened early in the morning, and the Lord gave me a word for a dear friend. The word was about Mother's Day and the prophetic anointing that would be on her life. I sent what the Lord revealed in a text message. She told me later that she operated in one of the most powerful releases of the prophetic. The word gave her confidence to step into the anointing that the Lord had placed in her life. Many times people know what they are supposed to do, but they need a word to minister to their current situation.

2. Confirmation—establishes and strengthens, builds faith and removes doubt. An example of a word of confirmation is "you are on the right track."

3. Future—speaks to next phase or stage in your life. This kind of word may map out directions or areas of preparation needed for future tasks. This can include instruction on what to do. God's words light our paths, so we know where to go.

4. Past—these are words that deal with past issues, often bringing understanding and resolving things from the past. These words help launch us into our future. There are many people chained to the past, and they need to be released. Joseph understood his past was necessary for his purpose to his people.

5. New—a new word is something completely new. It may often surprise the recipient. It is usually something they were not thinking or planning. Many people believe that prophecy must only confirm what the Lord has been speaking to you. (See 1 Corinthians 2:9–10.)

6. Warning—these words warn of dangers that may be ahead and what to avoid. An example is Agabus warning Paul of what he would face in Jerusalem (Acts 21:9–11).

7. Deliverance—these words deliver people from things such as hurt, rejection, fear, and sickness, and they release healing and restoration to the recipient (Ps. 107:20). These words are able to root things out of our lives (Jer. 1).

8. Revelation—these words give us insight and revelation into the plans and purpose of God for our lives (Deut. 29:29).

9. Identification—these words identify and help people understand and know who they are and who God created them to be (Judg. 6:12).

10. Correction—these words correct us and cause us to make the necessary adjustments in our lives (Prov. 3:11).

11. Commendation—God commends us when we are doing what is right. Each church in Revelation was commended and then corrected (Rev. 2–3).

12. Exposure—these words expose and identify the works of sin and darkness (Heb. 4:13).

13. Conditional—these words are conditional on your obedience. An example would be, "If you will pray and seek My face, then I will move you into a new level of breakthrough and blessing." This prophetic word is partial, progressive, and conditional. Many people trust the sovereignty of God in an unbiblical way. If a prophetic word reveals that you are called to be a nurse, you must go to nursing school to get skill

and knowledge. God is not going to make you a nurse by osmosis. Open up your brain and pour nursing skill into your head. We must remember that we are laborers *with* God.

14. Workmanship—These are words that deal with the sovereign work of God as Creator in your life. These words promote patience and endurance in the process of growth development. (See Ephesians 2:10.)

15. Judgment—these words declare and release judgment against wickedness.

16. World events—these words predict things that will come on nations and affect the world. This can be positive or negative. (See Acts 11:28.)

17. Sung—prophecy can be spoken or sung. These prophecies are usually accompanied by music and can touch a person deep inside. Through the power of singing and music (2 Sam. 23:1–2), these words release the beauty of the Lord. This can also be a song of love, giving us a greater revelation of God's love for us.

> The LORD thy God in the midst of thee is mighty; he will save, he will rejoice over thee with joy; he will rest in his love, he will joy over thee with singing. [These songs are called the song of Lord sung under the inspiration of chief musician.]
>
> —ZEPHANIAH 3:17

Any one of these words can be spoken over individuals, congregations, and nations. We must be open and allow God to speak to us in these different ways. Each way will bring great blessing to the church.

God Communicates to Us in Different Ways

God can speak to prophets and prophetic people in different ways. God is often speaking in different ways and man does not perceive it. Here are some of the different ways God speaks:

Impressions

This is an idea, feeling, or opinion about something or someone, especially one formed without conscious thought or on the basis of little evidence.

Still small voice

> And after the earthquake a fire; but the LORD was not in the fire: and after the fire a still small voice.
>
> —1 KINGS 19:12

The Lord normally speaks in the still small voice. On rare occasions He speaks with the audible voice. During the time of my prophetic training, I would hear other prophets exclaim about how the Lord spoke to them audibly. Many said He spoke to them in their right ear (it's always the right ear). They said He called them by name, and so on. I would always listen for an audible voice and became very discouraged and thought maybe I wasn't called to the prophetic.

I sought the Lord, and He used the parable of a mother who calls her children inside for dinner. The first time her voice is soft and sweet: "Johnnie, come in, honey. Wash your hands. It's time to eat." The second time her voice is firm, using more authority: "I said it's time to eat." By the third time the child hasn't responded, so distracted by all of the fun he's having. The mother's pitch is now elevated, using the child's full name: "Jonathan Tyrone Brown, I said get in here right now!"

The Lord told me that those who proclaim to hear the voice of

God audibly are generally rebellious and hard of hearing. He said He has to use extreme measures to get their attention. Sons of God are led by the Spirit of God. Hearing the audible voice every day is not the norm. This is how many open themselves up for error and deception.

Visions

Visions can be a revelation with the spirit eye or an open vision, which is like watching a scene with your eyes open. The natural surroundings blend into the overall scene. An example of this would be Moses seeing the burning bush (Exod. 3:1–6).

Visions need very little interpretation, but they require careful proclamation and application.

The prophets of God could understand God's council so clearly because He revealed matters to them by visible means.

- Isaiah—the entire sixty-six books of Isaiah were received in a vision.

- Ezekiel saw the heavens open and saw visions of God. Divine encounters that flooded Ezekiel's heart filled him with a faith and hope message for a people in captivity.

- Jesus said He saw what His Father was doing (John 5:19).

Dreams and vision that are from God root deep into our hearts, never to be forgotten. Dreams can sustain you through testing trials. The apostle Paul's defense to those who thought he was a heretic was that he was not disobedient to the heavenly vision.

> But rise, and stand upon thy feet: for I have appeared unto thee for this purpose, to make thee a minister and a witness both of these things which thou hast seen, and of those things in the which I will appear unto thee.
>
> —ACTS 26:16

Dreams

God often speaks this way because we are resting and not overwhelmed with the affairs of this life. Dreams can provide answers and even direct kings. Dreams can also warn us of impending danger (Matt. 2:12–13, 19, 22) and even keep us from death (Gen. 20:3–8). Dreams can also keep us from pride (Job 33:14–18) Dreams are messages that are sealed with parables. They are like snapshots that capture one brief moment in one lifetime. The dreamer is carried from scene to scene either as an observer or a participant.

Not every dream is from the Lord. Below you will find guidelines to discern the true from the false.

- Does the prophetic vision or dream reinforce God's Word, lead you to Christ, and fill you with love for the church?

- Does the prophetic vision or dream align itself with the clear teaching and doctrine of the Bible?

- Does the prophetic vision or dream strengthen your faith and give you an honorable purpose in life?

- Does the prophetic vision or dream turn you from wrongdoing, promoting righteousness and purity in the church?

- Does the prophetic vision or dream find wide acceptance and notable affirmation by notable men and women of God?

- Does the prophetic vision or dream build up the body of Christ by equipping believers for the work of the ministry?

Television

It is interesting that it is called *tele-vision*. Many times the Lord will have me, as a prophetic intercessor, to watch television to gain knowledge of what's happening in the city. I have received the burden of the Lord just from hearing other people's plights. The burden of the Lord can be described as an awakening in your spirit to the heart and desire of the Lord. In this context the Lord will alert you, as an intercessor, to His heart for a situation to pray His answer or solution to help the human condition.

When you pray the will of God, the prompt or heaviness lifts and you can go back to your normal life activities. Many prophets and prophetic people fall into a pitfall of the devil to carry around false burdens. They let the original God-given burden move them over into the soulish realm instead of keeping it in the spirit. Jesus said, "My yoke is easy and my burden is light" (Matt. 11:30). We must position ourselves as prophetic intercessors and mediators between heaven and earth to receive the burden of the Lord for our generation. This will open up supernatural realities for our generation.

Newspapers (world events)

The news keeps us abreast of what is happening in our world, and God is concerned about the world. He guides and intervenes in the affairs of men.

Trances

Trances are like dreams, but you are awake. It is a state of partial or complete detachment from your surroundings. You are aware of when you leave and when you return. (See Acts 10:10). "He hath said, which heard the words of God, which saw the vision of the Almighty, falling into a trance, but having his eyes open" (Num. 24:14).

Circumstances

Often natural circumstances can be opportunities for God to speak to us.

Preached messages

The word of God is prophetic, and preaching can also be a way that God speaks to us.

Divine decree

The Lord will sometimes use a divine decree to activate and turn the events of this world so they line up with the embedded commands and programs of the Lord.

Prophetic drama

The Lord will sometimes portray His word in live action, set to music or dance, depicting the invisible activities of eternity in public theatrics to demonstrate what He is doing behind the scene.

Weather

Wind, snow, rain, cold, and heat can all be prophetic symbols and signs to confirm the message of the messenger.

While ministering in Johannesburg, South Africa, I began to declare that the rain was coming as a sign of the showers of blessing that would come upon the church in South Africa. One of the prophets and dear friend said to me with great respect and concern, "Prophetess, it's not the season for rain." But on the last day after the last message was preached, God sent the rain as sign to people, confirming His message to His people.

Sign and wonders

God speaks through an event or wonder that hints to a deeper meaning. Signs and wonders serve to also confirm that God's hand is with His messengers (Mark 16:19–20). I experienced this while in South Africa. The Lord spoke to me through the sign of His rainbow and rain confirming His message and releasing faith in the hearts of His people. (See chapter 2.)

Chapter 10

Seek to Excel in Prophecy

*Pursue love, and desire spiritual gifts, but especially that you may
prophesy.... Even so you, since you are zealous for spiritual gifts,
let it be for the edification of the church that you seek to excel.*

—1 CORINTHIANS 14:1, 12, NKJV

HE LIFE OF the New Testament church is intended to be blessed
by the gift of prophecy. The proper placement of prophets
and prophecy in the body of Christ empowers the church
to accomplish more while expending less energy. Every word that
relates to prophetic gifts and their operation in the church requires
the believer to take initiative and responsibility to function. Paul
admonishes believers to desire, to covet, to stir up, to seek, and to
excel in prophecy for the edifying of the body of Christ.

Christianity is mostly proactive. If we are going to see the power
of God released in our generation, Christians must learn to take
the initiative to seek and to excel. To *excel* is to be preeminent or to
be at a level higher than another or others. There must be a higher
level of excellence in prophetic ministry. The prophet Daniel was
ten times better than the magicians of Babylon.

Many times Christians trust the sovereignty of God in a nonbib-
lical manner. Many believe that if the Lord wants to give them a
word to speak, He will just do it. God can give you a prophetic word
to encourage someone, but you must learn to co-labor with Him.
We must covet to prophecy. *Covet* is a passionate, active word. It is

the Greek word *zēlōtēs*, meaning one burning with zeal, a zealot.[1] It is used of God as jealous of any rival and sternly vindicating His control. *Covet* means to be most eagerly desirous of, zealous for, a thing to acquire a thing (zealous of). It also means to defend and uphold a thing, vehemently contending for a thing.

Paul admonishes Timothy, "Do not neglect the gift that is in you, which was given to you by prophecy with the laying on of the hands of the eldership. Meditate on these things; give yourself entirely to them, that your progress may be evident to all" (1 Tim. 4:14–15, NKJV).

Notice that if you're going to be excellent in ministering the spiritual gifts, you must give serious attention to the development of the gift. The Amplified Bible states that we should "Practice and cultivate and meditate upon these duties; throw yourself wholly into them [as your ministry], so that your progress may be evident to everybody" (v. 15).

Cultivating the Gift of Prophecy

The first major way to cultivate the gift of prophecy is to study the biblical definitions on how the gift functions and what role it plays in building the church. It is important to study the foundational principles of the prophetic found in the Bible. Paul writes that we should not be ignorant of spiritual gifts (1 Cor. 12:1). Ignorance is the number one reason the church is not walking in the fullness of the Spirit. Scripture tells us that the people are destroyed because of a lack of knowledge (Hosea 4:6). Ignorance destroys the proper placement of prophets and prophetic gifts in the body of Christ.

> But solid food belongs to those who are of full age, that is, those who by reason of use have their senses exercised to discern both good and evil.
>
> —HEBREWS 5:14, NKJV

Second you must practice, exercise, and use your spiritual senses. The phrase "reason of use" comes from the Greek word *hexis*, which means to practice and develop a habit.[2] We must develop a habit of using our spiritual senses.

We are born from heaven above by the Spirit of God, so we are not just human. We are also supernatural spirit beings. Exercising these spiritual senses, we learn to discern what Father God is speaking to us by His Spirit, and we cooperate with Him. By reason of use we train our spiritual senses to discern between good and evil, and by reason of use our spiritual senses can make distinction between good and God. When Eve saw that the tree was good, she ate (Gen. 3:6). Most times it's the good things that lead many away from God.

When God breathed His breath of life into Adam, He imparted the ability to function in the spirit realm (Gen. 2:7). The breath of life refers to life in the physical and spiritual realms. We were created to function in two worlds. Humanity was intended to live in two different realms—the natural realm relating to the earth and the spiritual realm relating to God. We are triune beings. We are spirit; we possess a soul and live in a body.

> And may the God of peace Himself sanctify you through and through [separate you from profane things, make you pure and wholly consecrated to God]; and may your spirit and soul and body be preserved sound and complete [and found] blameless at the coming of our Lord Jesus Christ (the Messiah).
>
> —1 THESSALONIANS 5:23, AMP

When Adam and Eve disobeyed God, it wasn't just a fall—it was spiritual death. Jesus was the Second Adam restoring everything back to us. The new birth experience restored the ability to operate in the natural physical realm and spiritual realm. We are now spiritual babies and must learn how to exercise and develop our spiritual sense.

The third way you can have your spiritual senses exercised in prophecy is to partner with a proven prophet to teach, train, and activate the gifts within you. Jesus ascended on high and gave gifts to men. He gave prophets for the equipping of the saints. A major role of prophets is to train and equip believers to function in prophecy.

> And He Himself gave some to be apostles, some prophets, some evangelists, and some pastors and teachers, for the equipping of the saints for the work of ministry, for the edifying of the body of Christ.
> —EPHESIANS 4:11–12, NKJV

Samuel, who was established and had a good report in the eyes of all Israel as a prophet of the Lord (1 Sam. 3:19–20), organized the prophets into a society for common instruction and edification. He established schools for the prophets, where men were trained in things pertaining to accountability, integrity, and scriptural accuracy. The students were generally called "sons of the prophets" (1 Kings 20:35; 2 Kings 2:3, 5, 7; 4:1, 38; 9:1). Such schools were established at Ramah (1 Sam. 19:19–20), Bethel (2 Kings 2:3), Jericho (2 Kings 2:5), and Gilgal (2 Kings 4:38). The members seem to have lived together as a society (2 Kings 6:1–4).

If you're going to excel in prophecy, it is important to be connected to a mature prophet. Training with a proven prophetic company that has a good report is paramount. The Bible says that "as iron sharpens iron, so one man sharpens another" (Prov. 27:17, NIV). The necessity of a prophet being proven in the local church is important. The concept of having a good report comes from the Greek word *martureo*, meaning to bear witness, give testimony.[3]

> The hearing ear, and the seeing eye, the Lord hath made even both of them.
> —PROVERBS 20:12

The year 2012 is a year of God releasing greater revelation and demonstration of Proverbs 20:12. We were made to hear the voice of God. Our ears were created to hear His voice, and our eyes to see His actions in our lives. Jesus clearly stated that "he can only do what he sees his Father doing" (John 5:19, NIV). It was never the will of God for man to dwell in darkness about His plans and purpose for our lives. He always wanted fellowship and relationship. The Lord wants His people to be filled with knowledge of His will in wisdom and spiritual understanding.

> For this reason we also, from the day we heard of it, have not ceased to pray and make [special] request for you, [asking] that you may be filled with the full (deep and clear) knowledge of His will in all spiritual wisdom [in comprehensive insight into the ways and purposes of God] and in understanding and discernment of spiritual things.
> —COLOSSIANS 1:9, AMP

Understanding the Deep Things of God

> But as it is written, Eye hath not seen, nor ear heard, neither have entered into the heart of man, the things which God hath prepared for them that love him. But God hath revealed them unto us by his Spirit: for the Spirit searcheth all things, yea, the deep things of God.
> —1 CORINTHIANS 2:9–10

Notice Paul begins this verse stating man's inability in the natural realm to understand the deep things of God. The word *search* denotes the process of investigation; the Holy Spirit searches and investigates the deep predetermined plans of God for each individual situation. The Holy Spirit reveals these plans and purposes of God to our spirit. The word *reveal* comes from the Greek word *apokalyptō*, which means to uncover, unveil, disclose.[4] It is a picture of something suddenly being removed, and obscure things are now in plain sight.

When the Holy Spirit lifts the veil from your spiritual eyes, ears, and heart, you can perceive truth that was veiled from your understanding. This is called revelation. Webster defines *revelation* as "the act of disclosing or discovering to others what was before unknown to them." It is the communication of truth to men by God through His authorized agents—the prophets and apostles. Revelation must be interpreted correctly before its application.

There is a connection between the eyes and the ears being open to the Holy Spirit, which allows the heart to comprehend.

The prophetic word or revelation comes through three basic spiritual senses: the eyes, the ears, and the heart. We have the ability to hear the voice of God. He opens our sight to see from His perspective and touches our hearts to feel as He does. Some people can even smell in the Spirit. Just as we have natural senses, we also have parallel spiritual senses.

Spiritual sight

Vision is the matrix of prophecy. Prophecy is the speaking forth of that which one sees and hears in the realm of the spirit. It is the articulation of the visions of God. The ministry of prophecy should always build up the church faith toward God and the Lord Jesus Christ by articulating the vision of the Lord. This enlarges the people's understanding of His greatness.

Prophetic people are given eyes to see from heavenly perspective (2 Kings 6:17). Prophets have an anointing from God to cause scales to be removed from their eyes to see the invisible. They give insight into spiritual issues, causing you to see that there is more with you than against you.

> And Elisha prayed, and said, Lord, I pray thee, open his eyes, that he may see. And the Lord opened the eyes of the young

man; and he saw: and, behold, the mountain was full of horses and chariots of fire round about Elisha.

—2 KINGS 6:17

Spiritual ears to hear

One of the most spoken admonishments from the Lord Jesus was "he that hath ears, let him hear." The Old Testament word for *hear* is *shama'*, meaning to listen and obey.[5] Our spiritual ears have to be awakened to hear the voice of the Lord that we may have the tongue of the learned to speak His wisdom and to comfort our generation (Isa. 50:4).

An understanding, listening heart

Solomon had greatness of understanding and largeness of heart. Largeness of heart is the ability to perceive—ability to understand beginning, middle, and end of a situation all at once. The Lord gave him a supernatural ability to see the whole picture (1 Kings 4:29).

> He also has planted eternity in men's hearts and minds [a divinely implanted sense of a purpose working through the ages which nothing under the sun but God alone can satisfy].
>
> —ECCLESIASTES 3:11, AMP

Solomon also asked for an understanding heart.

> Give Your servant an understanding heart that to judge Your people to discern between good and evil.
>
> —1 KINGS 3:9, NAS

In this passage understanding heart is translated as listening heart. This phrase literally means a heart that listens to God to accomplish what He has assigned.

How to Receive and Release a Prophetic Word

Eli taught Samuel how to discern, respond, and become sensitive to the voice of God. Prophets can only teach you how to cooperate with the activity of the Spirit, not how to manufacture the Holy Spirit's activity.

1. Put on your priestly garments. Priestly dimension must return to prophetic people. Prophetic people must put on their priestly garments and spend quality time in the presence of God, understanding their responsibility to minister to God and then to His people. Worshipping God for the testimony of Jesus is the spirit of prophecy. Worship is the doorway to the receiving the revelation from God. The apostle John paints a prophetic picture of the lifestyle of a prophetic minister (John 21:20). This verse shows how we must lay our head on the breast of Jesus and listen to the rhythm of His heartbeat being filled with the breath of God. We, in turn, breathe onto others the breath and life received from encountering the Creator. We must develop relationship and fellowship with the God who knows everything and about everything.

2. All of the Lord's words, no matter in what form we hear them, must be quickened and revealed by the Holy Spirit. *Quicken* means adding life to ordinary words. The Greek word for *quicken* means to make alive and give life by spiritual power to arouse and invigorate. The word Jesus speaks has life and vitality. Other words are just dead language. The message can come in a variety of ways—flashes of pictures, Scripture verses, sentence fragments, or impressions.

3. Activate faith to operate in the gift of prophecy much as you activated your faith to receive the gift of salvation. You prophesy according to the portion of your faith. The word *proportion* refers to a ratio. You can have faith to prophesy to one person or faith to prophesy to one hundred people. It's all based on the proportion of your faith. The apostle Paul challenged Timothy to stir up (rekindle and arouse from dormancy) the gift that was given to him (2 Tim. 1:6).

4. Ask, seek, and knock (Matt. 7:7–11). We can ask God for a prophetic word. Many are afraid to initiate conversation with the heavenly Father because of fear of deception or demonic interference. Notice Jesus states if you ask the Father for gifts, He will not give you something contrary to what you ask. God our Father, who is so in love with human beings, loves to hear the sound of a human voice asking and inquiring of Him. Jeremiah 33:3 says, "Call to Me, and I will answer you, and show you great and mighty things, which you do not know" (NKJV). *Mighty* comes from the Greek word *batsar,* which means secrets, mysteries, inaccessible things.[6]

5. God will immediately speak something to bless the body. God's first command was to bring light to chaos (Gen. 1:3). God speaks as a means to bring life and order. Since the moon and sun were not created until the fourth day, the light is the presence of illumination in general. Prophetic ministers should speak the light to every dark situation.

6. Focus is the key. Look in the spirit. Ask yourself, "What do I see, feel, or have a knowing about the situation?" God speaks through your spirit. It sounds like you. (See Isaiah 21:3–4.)

7. God will quicken one sentence, word, picture or thought to your spirit. Then you must exercise your faith to release the revelation given. It is like a piece of string on a sweater. Give it one pull and let the words flow. Open your mouth wide, and God will fill it (Ps. 81:10). The Holy Spirit will not move your mouth or override your will. You must give voice to what He is speaking.

8. Manifestation of the spirit is given to every man. *Manifestation* means to see and behold, to gaze by voluntary observation. It is to inspect, to appear, to discern, to clearly see, to experience, to perceive, to uncover, lay bear, reveal. It is also to open to sight, signifying shining. (See 1 Corinthians 12:7.)

9. The end result of prophecy is to find a way to put honor and glory back on mankind and restore what we lost in the garden—relationship to the Father. Everyone wants his or her crown of glory and honor. People are made for validation, celebration, and appreciation. "What is man that You are mindful of him, and the son of [earthborn] man that You care for him? Yet You have made him but a little lower than God [or heavenly beings], and You have crowned him with glory and honor" (Ps. 8:4–5, AMP.)

10. Prophecy releases the power of God, but don't let that be the center of attention. The focus is the heart of God being rightly communicated (1 Sam. 2:35).

11. God will give you a signal in your spirit to what He is about to do. I call them feelers. You will know when to look, listen, and release.

12. God does not just manifest words; He manifests Himself, so do not quench your emotions. Recognize

His thoughts in your mind. We must focus. We have the mind of Christ (1 Cor. 2:16).

13. Recognize the voice of the Lord. God drops things into your spirit, and they manifest on the screen of the spirit called the imagination. Because the Lord speaks through your human spirit, the voice sounds like your voice. It's not normally an outside voice, but the Lord will quicken words to your human spirit, and the voice sounds like you. God speaks through your personality. God will add life to ordinary words, experiences, and things that you can relate to. Jesus said, "It is the spirit that quickeneth; the flesh profiteth nothing: the words that I speak unto you, they are spirit, and they are life" (John 6:63). Words that are given by the Holy Spirit give life to what would otherwise be dead language.

Revelatory Gifting of the Prophet

Discerning of spirits

Discerning of spirits is supernatural insight into the realm of the spirit. *Discern* means to separate out mixture, to reveal truth. It is not suspicious. It reveals the type of spirit behind a person, a situation, an action, or a message. It is knowing in the spirit supernatural revelation concerning the source, nature, and activity of any spirit. There are three areas of activity to see into:

1. The spirit of God

2. The human spirit

3. Satan's kingdom

Both Jesus (Matt. 16:16–23) and Paul used their prophetic gifting to discern spirits.

> And it came to pass, as we went to prayer, a certain damsel possessed with a spirit of divination met us, which brought her masters much gain by soothsaying: The same followed Paul and us, and cried, saying, These men are the servants of the most high God, which shew unto us the way of salvation. And this did she many days. But Paul, being grieved, turned and said to the spirit, I command thee in the name of Jesus Christ to come out of her. And he came out the same hour.
>
> —ACTS 16:16–18

Once Paul discerned the spirit of this woman, he was able to speak to that spirit and command it to leave her. Because of how he used his prophetic gift, he was able to minister deliverance.

In evangelism we need to set the captives free. We need to be able to discern right and wrong spirits, to know how they have attached themselves, and to understand how they operate in a person's life. The key to discerning spirits is not insight based on our human nature, it is not based on what we see in the natural, and it is not a faultfinding tool. It is a ministry tool imparted by the Holy Spirit to set God's people free. Discernment is matured and increased as we grow in brotherly love (Phil. 1:9).

Word of knowledge

A word of knowledge is supernatural revelation revealed by the Holy Spirit of certain facts, present or past, about a person or a situation, which are not learned by the natural mind. An example of this would be a statement about someone's health, spiritual conditions, or location.

When a prophet or prophetic believer is ministering a word of knowledge, they have access to the facts in the mind of God about where someone is at the moment or an immediate need for a particular situation.

It is not amplified knowledge of what you already know (human knowledge). It is not knowledge based on your studies of the Word of God. It is not earned but given.

Word of wisdom

It is God's wisdom given to a person so they know to proceed in a course of action based on natural or supernatural knowledge. It's supernatural ability in the Spirit to impart special or specific information, guidance, or counsel, which brings life-changing illumination.

Directional

This is God telling you what to do, how to do it, the method of doing, and what is going to happen in the future. This is a flash of divine inspiration that is nearly always directed to the future. A great example of directional prophecy is found in Genesis 6:14–18, where the Lord gave Noah divine inspiration and direction for how to build the ark.

How the diversity of prophetic giftings can work together

In evangelism God can tell you through the word of knowledge about a complete stranger and then give you supernatural wisdom on how to proceed. It causes the unbeliever to be convinced that there is a living God who cares for him or her (1 Cor. 14:24–25).

A word of wisdom is given for protection and instruction and often reveals to us how to apply the knowledge that has been revealed.

As we are ministering in the prophetic, the word of wisdom may instruct us to:

1. Lay hands on a person

2. Speak a word of prophecy

3. Perform a creative miracle

4. Cast out a demon

5. Warn of danger and deliver from harm

How to operate in these revelatory gifts

A prophetic person must be motivated by the Holy Spirit to operate in the diversity of the prophetic gift. These various expressions are activated by the faith of the individual ministering and the one receiving ministry. The gifts work in accordance with our faith as ministers. Also, Jesus said many times that it was the person's faith that made them whole—well, healed, or delivered.

The diversity of the revelatory gifts can be manifested through impressions, thoughts, visions, and dreams.

Chapter 11

The Secret to Moving in Prophetic Timing

But I trusted in, relied on, and was confident in You, O Lord; I said, You are my God. My times are in Your hands; deliver me from the hands of my foes and those who pursue me and persecute me.

—PSALM 31:14–15, AMP

THERE IS NOTHING more important than time. Time is the measure of life. The quality of your life is determined by how effectively you use time. Actually you become what you do with your time. Time is an interruption of eternity. God created time and placed man it, but God doesn't live in time. Time was created to measure life and to take man out of eternity because eternity is timeless. Whatever happens in eternity lasts forever. It was grace and love that protected Adam in his sin state from eating from the tree of life unless he would have been an eternal sinner. You don't want to leave time without Jesus as your personal Lord and Savior.

Jesus reveals Himself as the Beginning and the End (Rev. 1:8). Totality rests in Him. Our time in life begins in Him and ends in Him. He is the A to Z. Jesus has already walked through our life. He has something for us to do every day. He fashioned our days before they ever existed (Ps. 139:16). Our times are in His hands. To everything there is a season, and to every purpose there is a time (Eccles. 3:1). God has a destiny for each one of His children, but we must learn to move our feet in perfect time.

As we begin to understand that our times, our days, and the plan for our lives are in the hands of God (Ps. 31:5), we can get a sense of how important it is to hear from Him concerning that plan. Knowing what God has planned for your life and how He wants you to live out His plan is part of the prophetic advantage. You have access and can know how to get your feet in perfect time. By the Spirit of God you can be at the right place at right time with the right people doing the right thing hearing the right message.

If you ask God to help you take inventory of where you are right now, how would you say your life is measuring up to the plan of God? Are you where you are supposed to be right now? Seriously, ask the Lord, "Am I where I should be according to Your plan for me?" This is a prophetic question. You do not need to be known as Prophet So-and-So to know the plan of the Lord for your life. The prophetic is for all God's people to walk in time with Him and His kingdom mandates.

We have to realize that the enemy also has a timetable for our lives that is contrary to God's timetable. The Bible says, "He shall speak pompous words against the Most High, shall persecute the saints of the Most High, and shall intend to change times and law. Then the saints shall be given into his hand for a time and times and half a time" (Dan. 7:25, NKJV). The devil is actively seeking to get us out of the timing of the Lord. He is trying to get us in places God never assigned us to be. We must realign ourselves with God's timing.

Sometime ago one of the most disturbing words from the Lord was spoken over me. It caused me to fall on my face. This was the word: "Michelle, you are seven years behind time." I immediately went into prayer and questioned the Lord, "Lord, I have been to over forty-five nations. I teach and train prophets, but You are telling me I am seven years behind time? What happened? What is going on?" He told me that I have been on ministry autopilot. He said that I had gotten caught up in comparing myself to other ministries and their leaders. When we get lost in comparison, we are focused on ourselves and are not drawing life from heaven and from God. We begin to take our times into our own hands. We use man as a comparison for where we should be or not be. But God says, "Look to Me for defining and perfecting your time. I have a divine growth schedule for you and your ministry."

Sometimes we can have so much revelation and go so many places ministering the word, healing the seek, bringing a word of hope and encouragement, but where does God say you should be right now? As believers in these last days, we can no longer be on ministry autopilot.

After I received that word and the Lord began to correct me and show me where I had gone wrong, I fell on my face and repented. I asked the Lord to accelerate the time in my life. I believe God is going to do that for many of us.

Accelerated Time

We are getting ready to move into a place of accelerated time. God is going to accelerate the timing in our lives. He is getting ready to orchestrate and put us in a place where the plowman will overtake the reaper.

> Behold, the days are coming, says the Lord, that the plowman shall overtake the reaper, and the treader of grapes him who sows the seed; and the mountains shall drop sweet wine and all the hills shall melt [that is, everything heretofore barren and unfruitful shall overflow with spiritual blessing].
>
> —Amos 9:13, AMP

What God is saying here is that the days or the time is coming when we will be pulling in the harvest before the plowman has a chance to till the field. This is talking about a supernatural redeeming of time (Eph. 5:16). The blessings and provision of God will be so much in these days that we will not be able to even sow.

The former and latter rain will come in the same season. God is doubling your time.

This will be a season of supernatural catching up and an acceleration for when we were out of time with God and not advancing and reaping as He had planned. He will do this for us because He is full of grace and mercy for His covenant children—those who seek after Him to know Him and to know His word for their lives.

The Father knows that we are dust and that some of the things we have decided on in our lives have put us in places that were not part of His plan. But He said that He is going to redeem our time. Instead of us having to go around the bend again because of our missteps, He is going to supernaturally accelerate us and put us back where we should have been all along. This is the season where "mercy and truth have met together; righteousness and peace have kissed" (Ps. 85:10)—putting us in the right place at the right time by His Spirit.

> And I will restore or replace for you the years that the locust has eaten—the hopping locust, the stripping locust, and the crawling locust, My great army which I sent among you. And you shall eat in plenty and be satisfied and praise the name of the Lord, your God, who has dealt wondrously with you. And My people shall never be put to shame.
>
> —Joel 2:25–26, AMP

God will create the same environment you missed and let you take advantage of opportunity one more time. God has an ability to re-create what you missed and let you take advantage of it again. Think about the story of Samson. He was foolish and moved out of the Spirit, but God let him do it one more time. He cried out to the Lord and asked Him to move upon him once again so he could destroy the Philistines, thus fulfilling his assignment as a deliverer of Israel (Judg. 16:28–30).

Once we have been accelerated, we cannot continue making

wrong moves. We have to make right decisions that keep us in the center of God's timing. To do this we have to pull back and spend time in the presence of the Lord. We have to consecrate ourselves, hear His voice, and listen for His instructions.

When we make sound decisions, every other option instantly becomes obsolete. Making sound decisions after your time has been accelerated is the same as repentance. You do not go back the same way you came after your course has been corrected, and you continue to stay in the vein so that His grace and mercy will fortify you for your assignment.

Understanding the Times

> So teach us to number our days, that we may gain a heart of wisdom.
> —PSALM 90:12, AMP

We must learn how to number our days to gain a heart of wisdom. Many think we have forever on the earth, but if we start measuring our life by days instead of years, we would use our days with wisdom and urgency to get the will of God accomplished.

- If you live for another 10 years, that equals 3,650 days.
- If you live for another 20 years, that equals 7,300 days.

Numbering your days breaks procrastination and awakens us to how we should spend time here on earth. To be awakened is to be aroused from dormancy. It is a renewal of interest, to recognize or realize, to quicken. We must be awakened to align for our assignment. *Alignment* is the arrangement in a straight line, a position of agreement or alliance. Many never see the prophetic word fulfilled because they never align properly to the word of the Lord.

If you look throughout the Bible, there are many passages that talk about wise men and fools. God says a fool is one who cannot see the future and take advantage of it (Eccles. 10:14; James 4:14–15). He is too confident in himself.

> A reproof enters deeper into a man of understanding than a hundred lashes into a [self-confident] fool.
>
> —PROVERBS 17:10, AMP

God is releasing prophetic seers and prophetic timers—people who are going to understand the times, who are going to understand what God is saying, who are going to understand how to take advantage of opportunities. Paul recognized the opportunities of the Lord and moved accordingly.

> For a wide door of opportunity for effectual [service] has opened to me [there, a great and promising one].
>
> —1 CORINTHIANS 16:9, AMP

He also recognized that there is an enemy of our souls who seeks to devour and steal our opportunities, changing the times.

> …and [there are] many adversaries.
>
> —1 CORINTHIANS 16:9, AMP

There are times when we will have to war to stay in the timing of God. We cannot just let the devil change our times.

Discerning the times and seasons of God is a skill all leaders must take advantage of.

> And of Issachar, men who had understanding of the times to know what Israel ought to do, 200 chiefs; and all their kinsmen were under their command.
>
> —1 CHRONICLES 12:32, AMP

Understanding of the times means to catch the wind of the Spirit, to discern the wind and to catch it. *Understanding* means to direct and separate mentally, to see the picture to take advantage of the season. Do you know why Donald Trump and Warren Buffett are so rich? They understood the time and began to take advantage of the season. When God begins to move in our lives, there will be times when we know the heavens are open and we can feel the presence of God. But what do we do? We just pray in tongues and roll on the floor and laugh instead of getting in God's presence and getting some instructions on how to advance in that season.

God grows everything according to the basic principle of seedtime and harvest (Gen. 8:22). Every prophetic word has to go through four seasons before harvesttime—spring, summer, fall, and winter. One of the major reasons many believers become stagnated and stuck in their walk with the Lord is because they don't understand the seasons in their lives. We need to learn how to work with God's timing and not against it. God is a God of seasons. He's a God of cycles and seasons and patterns and sequence. We cannot continue to build and do things out of sequence.

If we are going to build and grow according to the timing of the Lord, we will need to do it from a place of righteousness. Certain people with certain hearts, those who have been in the presence of the Lord, will be able to take advantage of the seasons to direct, to inform, to instruct, to see, and to perceive. They will not only understand the times, but they will also know what to do and when to do it. It will take these spiritually minded people who move in the principles of the kingdom to operate in the fruit of the Spirit and really be in a place where God speaks.

> The Lord by skillful and godly Wisdom has founded the earth; by understanding He has established the heavens. By His knowledge the deeps were broken up, and the skies distill the dew.
>
> —PROVERBS 3:19–20, AMP

We need the wisdom, or strategic skill, of the Lord to have a higher level of understanding of the times. He wants to give this to us without limit (James 1:5) so that we can be established and knowledgeable concerning our assignment.

How to Align With the Prophetic Timing of the Lord

It is going to take spiritually minded people to fulfill a mandate in these last days. Carnality must be removed. The spiritual mind is controlled by the fruit of the Spirit. It is a mind-set governed by kingdom principles. It is a mind set on life and peace.

The carnal mind, the mind of the flesh, or the soulish mind is at enmity with God. These are thoughts that originate with:

- Lust of flesh—natural appetites or desires that all humans have

- Lust of the eye—the desire to have things of the world as necessities

- Pride of life—a success spirit; position plus power plus prestige equal status symbols

> Now the mind of the flesh [which is sense and reason without the Holy Spirit] is death [death that comprises all the miseries arising from sin, both here and hereafter]. But the mind of the [Holy] Spirit is life and [soul] peace [both now and forever]. [That is] because the mind of the flesh [with its carnal thoughts and purposes] is hostile to God, for it does not submit itself to God's Law; indeed it cannot.
>
> —ROMANS 8:6–7, AMP

The Holy Spirit is the one who will guide us into knowing what the Lord is saying to us during this season. He gives divine illumination to the timing of the Lord.

> I have still many things to say to you, but you are not able to bear them or to take them upon you or to grasp them now.

But when He, the Spirit of Truth (the Truth-giving Spirit) comes, He will guide you into all the Truth (the whole, full Truth). For He will not speak His own message [on His own authority]; but He will tell whatever He hears [from the Father; He will give the message that has been given to Him], and He will announce and declare to you the things that are to come [that will happen in the future]. He will honor and glorify Me, because He will take of (receive, draw upon) what is Mine and will reveal (declare, disclose, transmit) it to you. Everything that the Father has is Mine. That is what I meant when I said that He [the Spirit] will take the things that are Mine and will reveal (declare, disclose, transmit) it to you. In a little while you will no longer see Me, and again after a short while you will see Me.

—JOHN 16:12–16, AMP

We must allow the Holy Spirit to give us the truth of what God has planned for us so that we can act on the right things when they come our way. When we are faced with certain decisions, God wants us to make choices based on what He has called us to do and not what we feel like doing. We can easily get out of line with His Spirit by doing what our carnal mind wants to do. But the Lord showed me that He will have to deal with the following five things in order for us to get in the right place at the right time according to His timetable for our lives.

1. Ambition

Until John came, there were the Law and the Prophets; since then the good news (the Gospel) of the kingdom of God is being preached, and everyone strives violently to go in.

—LUKE 16:16, AMP

This verse is talking about the "zeal of the Lord" when it says that "everyone strives violently to go in." I call this godly ambition.

Some people don't care for the word *ambition*, but I'm not talking about selfish ambition. I believe that as we seek the Lord to align with Him, He is going to increase our godly ambition. He is going to strengthen our passion and our desire to walk according to His kingdom mandates. We have to let the mandate of God rise up out of us. We can no longer just sit back and wait for something to happen. We must understand that the time is now for us to do great things for God.

In Genesis 2:19 the Lord brought the animals before Adam, and He looked to see what Adam would name them. In our limited thinking, perhaps we imagine God bringing an animal to Adam and then whispering in his ear that animal's name: "That's an elephant. Call it an elephant, Adam." Then Adam says, "You shall be an elephant."

I don't believe that's how it happened at all. God made Adam in His image and likeness. Creativity was already inside him. Adam had full ability to operate in godly ambition and name the animals himself.

I believe that God is moving and changing the times to where we've been trained enough. We've been tested, and He's awakening our ability to act on our godly ambition. He is going to strengthen our hearts to strike out and act upon the mandate He has birthed within us.

God is saying, "Move out and do what I'm telling you to do. I will be with you. Creativity is on the inside of you because I am on the inside of you. Christ in you, the hope of glory. Start moving out." What's stirring in your heart? Christianity is proactive. God is going to deal with us and strengthen our godly ambition so that we know we already have permission to advance the kingdom.

2. Attitude

Blessed are the flexible, for they won't get bent out of shape. Don't let attitude get ungodly, because you will lose time. Offense stops your growth timing, but do not worry; the refiner's fire is coming.

We're getting ready to be placed in situations where it's going to take extreme patience. We will need a double portion of the fruit of the Spirit. We get a great shout and hallelujah when we say a double portion of the power of God. But a time is coming when we will need a double portion of the fruit of the Spirit to carry out our assignments.

God is refining us through everyday life situations such as offense. Offense interrupts development and movement. We have to get rid of offense.

God will allow our flesh to be offended to get the best out of our spirits. God will offend our minds to get the best out of our hearts.

3. Authority

God is helping us fine-tune our understanding of authority. He wants us to understand the difference between leadership and management. Once we get this understanding, we will be in place to receive the greater level of authority that He is releasing to His people, and we will know how to use it.

Are you moving in the gift of leadership, or are you in management? Are you casting vision? Are you giving instructions? Are you correcting what needs to be corrected in the church? In the Book of Ezekiel when the angels of the Lord came into the temple, they began to measure the house of God. They were measuring because God was ready to send the glory. I'm telling you God is measuring us in this time because He's ready to send His glory. He's ready to send His power. His move will not fail. His kingdom will advance, and it will advance with integrity.

Are you leading from a title, or are you operating and functioning regardless of whether man gave you a title or not? If God called you as a believer, don't apologize anymore. As a believer signs shall follow you. This is your authority in Christ: "In My name they will cast out demons; they will speak with new tongues; they will take up serpents; and if they drink anything deadly, it will by no means hurt them; they will lay hands on the sick, and they will recover" (Mark 16:17–18, NKJV).

Authority is not recognized until it is used. Use the authority God gave you to carry out the godly ambition He has called you to.

4. Assignment

Anointing increases when assignment is clear. God sends you time to fulfill your assignment, but when you make mistakes, you lose time. The more we play around and flirt around with our assignment, the more time it costs us. What has God assigned you to do? Who should you be by now? Ask Him to show you these things.

Then don't be religious when God opens up a door that doesn't look like the door you're used to going through. Don't be intimidated if it looks like something you feel you can't do. Obey God and think outside of the box.

A while back a door opened up for me that made me question if I should go. A woman invited me to a cocktail hour at a locally owned nightclub. Leaders from all over the city would be there. She asked me to come to pray for the couples who owned the nightclub and other friends of hers who were having problems. I immediately began to think, "What if some Crusaders see me? How can I get in there and get out without being seen?" I did decide to go and pray for the people. There were several influential leaders of the city there. Many of the them began asking me a series of questions: "Where is your ministry? Do you want to start something? How can we help you?" If I was not open to this "out-of-the-box" assignment, I would not have had access to such favor. Can somebody say, "Right place, right time"? This type of assignment requires a certain level of maturity. I don't recommend this to new believers or someone who's been delivered from the nightclub scene. Initially I was reluctant to take this assignment, but after prayer and counsel I stepped out in faith.

God wants to deal with our interpretation of what our assignment is. He wants us to be listening to Him and following Him where He leads and not where we think He would have us go. This is the finest hour of the prophets, but we have to be at the right place to stand on those platforms.

5. Application

When God gives you revelation, He will also show you how to apply it. In these last days a fresh revelation on how to minister to the multitude and how to bring in the harvest is coming.

God is going to show us how to bring in the multitude. He's getting ready to show you the significance of the passions of your heart and how they play into His ultimate plan for advancing the kingdom. The divine purpose and how to apply all that you were created to be is going to be revealed. When you begin to see the souls your passions are assigned to, and as you began to cry out from your innermost being, revival fires are going to come.

God has predetermined your times. The footsteps of a good man have been ordered (or established) by God (Ps. 37:23). There are certain things God has already established for you to get in agreement with, for you to experience in your life. Let this be a season where you get on those paths of righteousness according to the purpose of His will, according to the counsel of His will.

Right Time, Right Place

Second Kings 8 tells the story of the Shunammite woman. If you recall, she and her husband were having a hard time having a baby. They built a house for Elisha, and he blessed them and they had a baby. The son died. Elisha raised the baby up. Then there was a season of famine. When the famine came, Elisha told the family to leave the land. Then after the season of famine was up, he said go back.

> It came to pass, at the end of seven years, that the woman returned from the land of the Philistines; and she went to make an appeal to the king for her house and for her land. Then the king talked with Gehazi, the servant of the man of God, saying, "Tell me, please, all the great things Elisha has done." Now it happened, as he was telling the king how he had restored the dead to life, that there was the woman whose son he had restored to life, appealing to the king for her house and for her land. And Gehazi said, "My lord, O king, this is the woman, and this *is* her son whom Elisha restored to life." And when the king asked the woman, she told him. So the king appointed a certain officer for her, saying, "Restore all that was hers, and all the proceeds of the field from the day that she left the land until now."
>
> —2 KINGS 8:3–6

She followed the prophetic instructions: the prophet told her to leave and to come back in seven years. Then she walks in to the king's court at the same time Elisha's servant is telling her story to the king. God gave her favor, and the king gave her favor and all the money that she needed and her land—all this because she was obedient to the prophetic timing of the Lord. She was fully restored.

Every time we disobey the voice of the Lord, we miss a divine setup. God is always after our growth. He is always after promoting us to get to our destiny. He always wants us to move to a place of fulfillment. He always wants us to have exceedingly abundantly above all we can ask or think. He's always about the abundance. But if every time we are not where He tells us to be, we miss a divine setup.

God is a divine chess player. He is the master chess player. He likes to move us around, put us in certain places, so we can be the winner of the game. He is the wise master builder. As I said, your times are in His hands.

God is teaching us how to move with Him. He is pouring out His glory so we understand Him and love Him, so we can't be bought and there are no more strings tying us to the things of this world. There will be a remnant of people who will know the timings of God. The sons of Issachar were one of the smallest tribes of Israel and "men that had understanding of the times" (1 Chron. 12:32).

This is a season that the glory and grace of God will rest upon you. You will begin to have face-to-face encounters with the Lord, and from that place of encounter the Lord is going to ignite your passion. He is going to bring you to a place of assignment and alignment. From that place of alignment nothing will be able to stop you. Even as the spirit of the fear of the Lord rests upon you, you will not fear man. You will be impregnated with destiny, so be mindful of your diet. Eat the meat of His Word and drink from His cup that never runs dry.

The Lord says, "I shall give My people eyes to see, and they will began to understand their purpose and their destiny as never before because their confidence is in Me. Their confidence is in My love."

Chapter 12

Angels and the Prophetic Word

*Bless the LORD, ye his angels that excel in strength, that do
his commandments, hearkening unto the voice of his word.*

—PSALM 103:20

THERE HAVE BEEN many books written on the subject of angels,
but I aim to connect the ministry of angels to the prophetic
word. Notice that angels hearken to the voice of God's word.
Angels excel in strength. Angels are powerful spirits who have been
sent to assist us in advancing the kingdom.

Are they not all ministering spirits, sent forth to minister for
them who shall be heirs of salvation?
—HEBREWS 1:14

It is important to know that we are not alone. Angels are ministering spirits sent forth to minster on our behalf. They give us
supernatural assistance.

Many who hear the word of the Lord wonder how it could ever
happen. It happens when God sends His angelic servants to help
fulfill His divine purposes. When we speak and decree the word of
God, they begin to minister on our behalf.

Angels are at work behind the scenes. They influence cities,
nations, governments, and history. Angels are also sent to minister
on the behalf of individuals. Angels are involved in helping you fulfill your destiny and purpose.

Churches also have angels on assignment. Angels help churches fulfill their destiny and purpose. Angels hearken to the prophetic utterances spoken over individuals and congregations.

> And he dreamed, and behold a ladder set up on the earth, and the top of it reached to heaven: and behold the angels of God ascending and descending on it.
>
> —GENESIS 28:12

Jacob saw a portal through which angels were ascending and descending. This portal is Bethel, the house of God and the gate of heaven. The house of God today is the church. We are now Bethel.

A portal to heaven is opened when we pray, praise, worship, preach, and prophesy. Angels ascend and descend through this portal. They are sent to help and assist us.

The Various Ministries of Angels

> And Jacob went on his way, and the angels of God met him. And when Jacob saw them, he said, This is God's host: and he called the name of that place Mahanaim.
>
> —GENESIS 32:1–2

Angels are connected to prophets and prophetic people. Jacob encountered a host of angels. These angels were assigned to bring Jacob to his designated place. In other words angels were a part of his fulfilling his destiny. *Mahanaim* in the verse above means "two camps."[1] This was an angelic army sent to assist Jacob.

The prophetic word reveals and releases destiny. God has a destiny for each person, and we are responsible to discover it, pursue it, and walk in it. Angelic assistance includes angels that go before us and angels that protect us. They assist us against human and demonic opposition. They assist us in overcoming resistance to the fulfillment of His word.

The chariots of God are twenty thousand, even thousands of angels: the Lord is among them, as in Sinai, in the holy place.

—Psalm 68:17

Angels were instrumental in the giving of the Law. They were involved in the establishment of the covenant between God and His people. Angels are always involved with God's covenant people. Those in covenant with God are not alone. We are not left to our own strength in fulfilling the word of the Lord.

Who maketh his angels spirits; his ministers a flaming fire.

—Psalm 104:4

Angels are spirits. They operate in the invisible realm. They are spiritual beings that respond to the word of the Lord. They respond to prayer, praise, worship, fasting, preaching, and prophecy. Spirits respond to spiritual activities.

And I will send an angel before thee; and I will drive out the Canaanite, the Amorite, and the Hittite, and the Perizzite, the Hivite, and the Jebusite.

—Exodus 33:2

Angels go before us to drive out the enemy. They go before us to make way for us to possess our possessions. The word of the Lord is often a declaration of what belongs to us. We are not alone in trying to possess it.

Angels help to provide significant breakthroughs. Angels help us overcome impossible odds. Angels help us to overcome giants and strong enemies.

The Prophetic Word Initiates the Activity of Angels

This can all begin with a prophetic word. The word initiates the activity of angels in our lives. I also believe that different angels can be assigned from heaven to us at different times.

> So shall my word be that goeth forth out of my mouth: it shall not return unto me void, but it shall accomplish that which I please, and it shall prosper in the thing whereto I sent it.
>
> —ISAIAH 55:11

> And he said unto me, The LORD, before whom I walk, will send his angel with thee, and prosper thy way; and thou shalt take a wife for my son of my kindred, and of my father's house.
>
> —GENESIS 24:40

Prosper means to succeed or flourish. God's word will prosper or succeed where it is sent. Angels can be sent before us to prosper our way. We can also prosper through prophesying (Ezra 6:14).

Prophetic intercession and prophetic utterances are instrumental in releasing the ministry of angels. God is committed to performing His word. He sends His angels to assist in its performance

> That confirmeth the word of his servant, and performeth the counsel of his messengers; that saith to Jerusalem, Thou shalt be inhabited; and to the cities of Judah, Ye shall be built, and I will raise up the decayed places thereof.
>
> —ISAIAH 44:26

God performs the counsel of His messengers. His messengers were the prophets. God is committed to His word, and He sends angels to cause it to come to pass.

> Then said the LORD unto me, Thou hast well seen: for I will hasten my word to perform it.
>
> —JEREMIAH 1:12

I love this verse of Scripture. God watches over His word to perform it. Angels excel in strength to do the will of God. God has made them strong for this purpose. Angels are involved in what God's messenger speaks. We do not have the strength or wisdom to do the great things God speaks. Man is limited in his power and ability to perform the counsel of God. We are dependent upon heaven and its resources.

We can trust God to release His angels on our behalf when we speak and walk in His counsel. Angels are given charge over us. In other words they are appointed over us. They assist us and protect us as we walk in God's purpose for our lives.

> For he shall give his angels charge over thee, to keep thee in all thy ways.
> —PSALM 91:11

Angels delight in hearing and fulfilling God's prophetic word. Angels take pleasure in assisting us to fulfill God's plans. They continually wait on God and His people. Angels love God's word, and they love performing it. Angels love God's presence, and they love to praise and worship Him.

> Be not forgetful to entertain strangers: for thereby some have entertained angels unawares.
> —HEBREWS 13:2

Angels visit our services, and it is possible that they have been there in the form of humans without us being aware.

Strong worship is an atmosphere for angels and the prophets. Heaven drops (Hebrew word *nataph*, meaning "to prophesy"[2]) at the presence of God (Ps. 68:8). Prophets and prophetic people also love God's presence and His word. Angels join us in our worship. They also listen to the word of the Lord.

> Unto whom it was revealed, that not unto themselves, but unto us they did minister the things, which are now reported unto

you by them that have preached the gospel unto you with the
Holy Ghost sent down from heaven; which things the angels
desire to look into.

—1 PETER 1:12

Angels have a great desire to look into the things God speaks.
They are interested in His prophetic plans and seeing them come to
pass. I believe they rejoice at the fulfillment of His word. Angels are
interested in seeing your prophetic words and destiny come to pass.
They enjoy its fulfillment.

Angels often stand behind prophets and ministry gifts when
they are preaching. We have seen this many times in our services.
Angels often stand on the platform. They are involved in what we
are preaching and declaring.

I send an Angel before thee, to keep thee in the way, and to
bring thee into the place which I have prepared. Beware of
him, and obey his voice, provoke him not; for he will not
pardon your transgressions: for my name is in him. But if
thou shalt indeed obey his voice, and do all that I speak; then
I will be an enemy unto thine enemies, and an adversary unto
thine adversaries.

—EXODUS 23:20–22

Do Not Provoke Angels

Angels can even be provoked. God warned Israel not to provoke
the angel sent before them. Disobedience to the word and voice
of the Lord can provoke angels. "Provoke" is the Hebrew word
marar, meaning to make bitter or make enraged.[3] This is a sobering
thought. Angels don't like when God's word is disobeyed. Angels
place high honor on the word of the Lord. They are committed to
God and His word.

And Elisha prayed, and said, LORD, I pray thee, open his eyes,
that he may see. And the LORD opened the eyes of the young

man; and he saw: and, behold, the mountain was full of horses and chariots of fire round about Elisha.

—2 KINGS 6:17

Angels are therefore absolutely committed to God's word and seeing it come to pass. They are faithful servants of God and faithful to us as well when we walk in and obey God's word. The prophet Elisha was aware of the heavenly host and prayed for God to open the eyes of his servant.

The Lord also opened the eyes of Balaam to see an angel in the way (Num. 22:31). This angel was sent to withstand Balaam, who was called by Balak to curse Israel. Balaam was spared and prophesied blessing over Israel, which enraged Balak.

We don't want to provoke angels. We want them on our side assisting us. They make great helpers but are formidable enemies. When we submit to God's prophetic purposes, they will be our friends and not our enemies. They will help us succeed and fulfill God's prophetic word and plan for our lives.

Angels Carry Out God's Judgments

And immediately the angel of the Lord smote him, because he gave not God the glory: and he was eaten of worms, and gave up the ghost.

—ACTS 12:23

When prophets prophesy judgment, then angels can be released to fulfill them. Angels assist in carrying out God's judgments. Individuals and nations can come under judgments executed by angels. God watches over His word to perform it. God can use human armies and angelic armies to release judgments. Angels are involved in the judgments released in the Book of Revelation.

For I will defend this city, to save it, for mine own sake, and for my servant David's sake. And it came to pass that night, that the angel of the LORD went out, and smote in the camp of the Assyrians an hundred fourscore and five thousand: and when they arose early in the morning, behold, they were all dead corpses. So Sennacherib king of Assyria departed, and went and returned, and dwelt at Nineveh.

—2 KINGS 19:34–36

An angel destroyed the camp of the Assyrians after Isaiah released the word of the Lord to Hezekiah. This was an immediate fulfillment. This again shows the power of angels and their obedience to the word of the Lord.

Prophets and prophetic people are connected to the angelic realm. The invisible realm responds to the spoken word. Our words are spirit and life. Prophetic words are the spiritual containers of the will and purposes of God. We need a greater understanding of the spirit realm and the power of prophecy. This understanding will help us walk in the fullness of the prophetic ministry and speak the word with boldness, expecting God to perform what He says through us.

Chapter 13

The Plumb Line

Thus he shewed me: and, behold, the LORD *stood upon a wall made by a plumbline, with a plumbline in his hand. And the* LORD *said unto me, Amos, what seest thou? And I said, A plumbline. Then said the* LORD, *Behold, I will set a plumbline in the midst of my people Israel: I will not again pass by them any more.*

—AMOS 7:7–8

PLUMB LINE IS a simple tool used to determine whether or not something is perfectly vertical—upright. However, there are things that are crooked that can never be made straight. False teaching and sexual perversion cannot be made straight in the sense that they cannot be justified or declared right. The prophet will see things that are crooked. The prophetic ministry is a plumb line ministry. Prophets are called to make crooked things straight, rough places smooth, valley areas of your life high, and mountain prideful areas low.

> That which is crooked cannot be made straight: and that which is wanting cannot be numbered.
>
> —ECCLESIASTES 1:15

> Consider the work of God: for who can make that straight, which he hath made crooked?
>
> —ECCLESIASTES 7:13

> Woe unto them that call evil good, and good evil; that put
> darkness for light, and light for darkness; that put bitter for
> sweet, and sweet for bitter!
>
> —ISAIAH 5:20

It is dangerous to justify evil and call it good. It is evil to call what is bitter sweet. God pronounced judgment upon those who did this. The prophet calls it what it is. There is no confusion in the mind of God concerning right and wrong, and neither should there be any confusion in our minds.

Ward, *watch*, and *watchman* are words that refer to a watch over a local church, region, state, or nation to preserve, protect, or guard.

Prophets are watchmen. They watch and pray. Prayer is an integral part of the prophet's ministry. Intercession is another aspect of the prophet's ministry. As watchmen prophets receive revelation in advance. They see what is coming before it comes. They prepare people for what is coming.

Intercession is to petition the Father on behalf of another person, a city, or a nation; prophetic intercession is discerning the wisdom of God about a person or situation and praying in agreement with the direction the Lord has revealed. Prophetic prayer is the highest form of intercession.

> But if they be prophets, and if the word of the LORD be with
> them, let them now make intercession to the LORD of hosts,
> that the vessels which are left in the house of the LORD, and
> in the house of the king of Judah, and at Jerusalem, go not to
> Babylon.
>
> —JEREMIAH 27:18

Jeremiah is challenging the false prophets to make intercession that Israel would not go into captivity. If they had the word of the Lord, they would not pray this because God had determined to take Israel into captivity. Prophets make intercession based on the word of the Lord.

And he cried, A lion: My lord, I stand continually upon the watchtower in the daytime, and I am set in my ward whole nights.

—ISAIAH 21:8

Ward is the Hebrew word *mishmereth*, meaning a place where guards are set; a station.[1] In other words Isaiah was placed in a station by God to watch God's purposes being fulfilled. He would watch whole nights.

And [the watchman] cried like a lion, O Lord, I stand continually on the watchtower in the daytime, and I am set in my station every night.

—ISAIAH 21:8, AMP

Prophets are spiritual watchmen set in the church by God. Every church needs watchmen. Watchmen protect and guard. Watchmen are concerned about the plans and purposes of God that are coming to pass. They can watch for judgment or watch to protect.

And by a prophet the LORD brought Israel out of Egypt, and by a prophet was he preserved.

—HOSEA 12:13

Another word that describes the prophet's ministry is the Hebrew word *shamar*. This word means to preserve or protect.[2] Adam was told to keep (*shamar*) the garden. The church is now the garden of the Lord, and we are called to protect it and guard it from the serpent. Israel was preserved by the intercession of Moses. Prophets help protect the church from the plans of hell through prophetic intercession.

So thou, O son of man, I have set thee a watchman unto the house of Israel; therefore thou shalt hear the word at my mouth, and warn them from me.

—EZEKIEL 33:7

Watchmen also warn of impending danger. They set the trumpet to their mouths to announce the sword is coming. They have a responsibility to blow the trumpet. The trumpet is the sound used to gather, to journey, and to warn. The voice of the prophet is like a trumpet.

> Blow the trumpet in Zion, sanctify a fast, call a solemn assembly.
>
> —JOEL 2:15

The prophet can blow the trumpet to call for repentance, fasting, and mourning when there is gross sin and iniquity. The heed to this call can save lives. God's voice is like a trumpet (Rev. 1:10).

> But if the watchman see the sword come, and blow not the trumpet, and the people be not warned; if the sword come, and take any person from among them, he is taken away in his iniquity; but his blood will I require at the watchman's hand.
>
> —EZEKIEL 33:6

The prophet feels a great responsibility to declare what he sees. He does not take what God shows him lightly. This can become what is called a burden. *Burden* is the Hebrew word *massa'*, meaning a prophecy of doom.[3] Judgment does not originate in the heart of a prophet. Judgment originates from God, and the prophet proclaims it.

I don't want to give the impression that all prophets do is prophesy doom and gloom, but this can be a part of the prophet's ministry. We must remember that old covenant prophets ministered primarily to people who were covenant breakers under the Law.

> I will stand upon my watch, and set me upon the tower, and will watch to see what he will say unto me, and what I shall answer when I am reproved.
>
> —HABAKKUK 2:1

The watchman waits for the word of the Lord. Habakkuk waited for a response to his complaint before God. Prophets can pray for insight and revelation and expect to receive a response. Prophets have questions. They are often perplexed by what they see in the natural, and they need an answer from heaven. This of course can refer to any believer, but it is especially true for prophets.

Prophets can also have questions about what the Lord shows them. They need interpretation. Some things are more difficult to understand than others. Daniel's visions were difficult for him to understand, and he needed an angel to answer his questions.

God's Word should always be elevated as the plumb line by which all prophetic ministry is measured.

Amos had a plumb line in his hand to measure the purity of Israel. We are to measure the purity and purpose of God with its complexities in the temple, altar, and its worshippers (Rev. 11:1). It will require true spiritual discernment.

A Prophet Must Be Measured

Before the prophet can fully and accurately walk in this plumb line anointing, he or she must first be measured. There is such a high level of evil and false teaching in the earth that the prophet must be found right and judged in the eyes of the Lord. If a prophet has not been measured, he or she risks ministering from a place of deception.

God assures His people that He will release prophetic direction and great power to them. They will understand God's heart and plans. The saints will prevail against deception at that time. In Revelation 10 God promised to raise up prophetic messengers. These prophets will have been tested and measured by the Lord before bringing understanding that helps people avoid deception. This passage is important for prophets and prophetic people to study.

In Revelation 10:9-11 the prophet is admonished to take the book, to eat the book, and then prophesy. Eating the book means embodying the message. The prophet and the message must be one. The message must go deep into the prophet's spirit before he can have authority to deliver it. The prophet must get intimately acquainted and become the message that God has given him to deliver. The prophet is the message, and the message is the prophet; they become one. The word of God that has been digested becomes the plumb line. The Word of God is the final authority in life whereby everything is measured.

Matthew tells us that in the last days the very elect will be deceived (Matt. 24:24). The thing about deception is that you don't always know how off you are. The devil starts releasing confusion in your mind, and you start saying a certain issue is complex and questioning what God says was absolutely wrong. You begin to think that maybe it is right. The power of deception is the person thinks he is right. You cannot convince a deceived person that he's off.

But when you've been measured by God and you are faced with those same issues, you can confidently say, "No, devil, that is deception." The Word of God becomes your measuring rod or plumb line.

Prophets must be careful to stay humble before God so that they can remain sensitive to the measuring of God. As a prophet what you say matters. People adjust their lives to your words. You must know that the Lord is your portion and that you have been sent from the presence of the Lord; therefore you must deliver His words the way He said them, with His expression. Prophets must understand the power of words. I have seen prophets and prophetic people make decisions and say things that create a domino effect for years, and people's lives are destroyed.

An understanding of the burden of the prophetic call can help to maintain the prophetic measuring rod or plumb line. Revelation 10:11 states, "You must prophesy again" (NKJV). This is unique language for our generation. Many things in the earth will not happen unless the prophets speak, declare, and announce. God is watching over His words to fulfill them. Prophets and prophetic believers must prophesy to the heavens, prophesy to the destiny of families, prophesy to the government, prophesy to the kings and people of the earth. Let the prophets speak!

The Prophet's Mission

We must consider the backdrop of the prophetic word and the prophet's offices. The Lord has a set time when He wants to speak to His people. Psalm 102 states that there is a set time to favor Zion. The word *time* in the passage comes from Greek word *kairos*, which is the appointed time of God.[4] When the seasons for something the Lord has upon the timetables of human history have arrived, He will send the prophet to announce and unlock His plan and purpose in the earth. This may be a season to:

- Activate and anoint a person into ministry office for service. The prophet Samuel made a prophetic announcement and impartation when he took a horn of oil and anointed David in the midst of his brothers. At that time the Spirit of the Lord came upon David in power (1 Sam. 16:13).

- Reveal spiritual insight for that moment, delivering fresh current words from God and interpreting Scripture for contemporary times.

- Impart spiritual understanding and new giftings (Rom. 1:11).

- Reiterate and confirm the mission and plans of leadership (Ezra 5:1–2).

- Establish the church in God's righteousness so they may live lives that exemplify the new creation and manifest the indwelling Christ (1 Thess. 4:1–12).

- Incite the fear of the Lord (Heb. 12:25–29).

- Release the power to perform. Every utterance from God through His mature prophets contains with itself the seed of His divine nature and potential of His creative power.

- Prepare the way for the visitation of the Lord (Luke 1:17).

- Motivate repentance toward God for the things once practiced and yet to be renounced and relinquished (Jon. 3).

God has an audience to whom He wishes to direct His thoughts. This may be an individual, the church, or the nations.

Here is the progression of the prophetic word as it is birthed from the heart of God delivered to His mouthpiece, the prophet, and communicated to the rightful audience:

1. There is an empowerment of the spirit to hear and deliver.[5]

2. The prophet receives a tangible mantlelike anointing.[6]

3. The prophet hears God's voice in different modes of reception. The modes of reception can be found in the Old Testament words designated to the prophet.[7]

    - *Nataph* means "to drop down as water, to fall in drops; to flow, drip, ooze, distill, trickle; to cause words to flow." It means to preach words by prophetic discourse. (See Ezekiel 21:2.)[8] God will drop His prophetic word in your spirit.

    - *Naba'* means "to cause to bubble up, hence to pour forth words abundantly."[9] This type of reception fills your belly and gushes out like a fountain.

- *Ro'eh* means "a visionary, a seer." It comes from the verb *ra'ah*, which means "to see," and can also mean to perceive, stare, discern. (See 1 Samuel 9:9.)[10] This mode of reception comes in pictures. The prophet will receive message through visions.

- *Chazon* is "a prophetic vision, dream, oracle, revelation; especially the kind of revelation that comes through sight, namely a vision from God." (See 2 Chronicles 32:32.)[11] This type of reception needs very little interpretation because God's counsel is revealed by visible means.

- *Massa'* means both "oracle" and "burden" (See Ezekiel 12:10).[12] "The oracle (lifting up of the voice) was a burden (lifting something physically) placed upon the prophet until the message was delivered." (See Jeremiah 23:33).[13] This mode of reception is for when you bear and carry the word of the Lord. The Lord imparts His burden and you carry it throughout the earth until the assignment is fulfilled.

4. There is a time and place selected by God for delivery. This can be for now or later, in public or private.[14]

5. The time and place may or may not have symbolic significance.[15]

6. A response by the audience is expected.[16]

7. The audience accepts, rejects, or neglects the word.[17]

8. Repentance, commitment, or reaffirmation will take place.[18]

The Prophet's Mandate

The mandate: To restore God's original order in the earth. The primary directive of prophets and prophecy is to cause the image and likeness of God to be formed in mankind. The devil hates that mankind is made in the image or likeness or resemblance of God. He uses devastating life experiences to distort and shame mankind. Prophets and prophetic ministers have the honor and privilege to encounter God and reveal His purpose to His creation, restoring dignity and reconciling men to the heart of God.

I love to prophesy to God's people. I know how it provides an advantage to life. It literally empowers one to fill your destiny. The Bible tells us where there is no prophetic revelation or vision, people cast off restraint (Prov. 29:18). The prophet's ministry should reveal the hope of God's calling in the lives of His creation.

The Prophet's Aim: What to Look For

When we begin to see with the eyes of the Lord, we will not see any situation or person as worthless or hopeless. When we begin to see with His eyes, we see potential in things that before were seemingly hopeless. One thing we must understand is that there are different characteristics of people. There are good people who are ready and pliable to receive prophetic ministry. There are bad people who will not believe and are not going to repent. Then there are broken people who really benefit from the power of prophecy that brings reconciliation, restoration, redemption, and dignity. These are the ones Jesus came to heal and deliver, and one of the tools He designed for this is prophecy.

Understanding means to put together, to mentally see the big picture, to comprehend what God is doing. It denotes the union and connection of a thing. Ephesians 1:17–18 states: "The God of our Lord Jesus Christ, the Father of glory, may give unto you the spirit of wisdom and revelation in the knowledge of him: The eyes of your understanding being enlightened; that ye may know what is the hope of his calling, and what the riches of the glory of his inheritance in the saints."

Enlightening the eye of our understanding will cause our hearts to be flooded with light. The prophets must have an enlightened eye of understanding so that they can deal with foundational and root issues in the lives of men and women.

> And now also the axe is laid unto the root of the trees: therefore, every tree which bringeth not forth good fruit is hewn down, and cast into the fire.
> —MATTHEW 3:10

We must focus our sight. In his prophetic vision Isaiah referred to the prophets as the eyes of Israel (Isa. 29:10). Through the Holy Spirit the prophets can "see" things regularly that others don't see.

Being prophetic is not about what you are looking at, but what you are looking for. Prophetic ministry must be able to take people to another place. They should not be left where they were found.

Prophecy Is Redemptive by Nature

Prophecy has the ability to take a person off the road of destruction to the path of righteousness. It can get them off the course of this world. It can break disobedience. Prophecy breaks down walls of petition that are standing between them and Christ. It does this in two ways.

1. Reconciliation

This is a word of prophecy that repairs the walls of petition, which can be rejection, abandonment, or anger toward God. To deliver this kind of word, the prophetic person should prophesy that the person has access out of the valley to the mountain. Many times prophetic words identify the problem; for instance, "My daughter, you have been rejected all your life, and now you feel rejected hurt and abandoned." The prophecy goes in this vein without any words spoken to deliver the person from rejection, but the person is already aware of their dejected state. The person manifesting rejection is hurting and crying without any access to the mountain of acceptance.

The prophet's word to a rejected person should be around acceptance, adoption, and the like. When the Lord reveals a heart condition, there is always an opposite word to bring the healing and deliverance.

2. Citizenship

People need to be connected to their foundation. The citizenship prophecy causes them to be fitly joined together. Prophets must remember that God is building a house, and they must beware of prophecies that promote elitism. These are the prophecies that sound something like this: "You are the one who will bring this church to a new level. You are the one." Loner prophecies promote a lone ranger mentality and isolation.

The prophetic person delivering this kind of word should prophesy and promote team ministry. There are many parts but one body. The Lord works in team ministry. One person doesn't have it all.

The Correction of the Lord Is Good

When there is a famine in the land, people will eat anything. There has been a famine of true authority and of the truth of the gospel being preached. I believe God is raising up true prophets who know the gravity of their assignment and will speak the truth in love and will not back down. They will let the Spirit of God measure them so that they can then create the atmosphere for the body of Christ to be ministered to and measured by God.

This chapter gives clear guidelines on how to function as a

prophetic plumb line to minister correction to God's people. God is serious about establishing His church. His divine plan for the body of Christ will not fail. We need not be afraid of His judgments. After the fire comes the glory. After the testings comes the power. After the correction comes the fulfilment.

Chapter 14

The Spirit and Power of Elijah

For David, after he had served his own generation by the will of God.

—ACTS 13:36

NEW COMPANY OF Elijah prophets are being equipped to restore the spiritual destiny of the church and our generation. God is raising a prophetic anointing that will help prepare the way for His purposes.

Here are questions we must ask ourselves:

- What prophet would God send to our generation?

- What prophet from the Bible would God send in the twenty-first century?

Our nation is in a progressive decline in morality. America's liberal abortion standards have allowed 50 million babies to be aborted since 1973.[1] Christian men are hooked on pornography. The homosexual agenda is gaining influence, and gay marriage is in the church. There is a sharp increase in divorce in the church. Human trafficking is the ugly side of globalization. Those who were once considered great leaders are preaching the doctrine of inclusion. Christian leaders are afraid to say on national television that Jesus Christ is the only way to salvation.

This sounds like a job for Elijah. His anointing challenged loyalty of the human heart faltering between opinions. In his day Elijah had to deal with Israelite kings who slowly succumbed to the influences of the culture around them. Elijah was anointed to break through four hundred years of religion and tradition, backsliding and hardness of heart.

As the Lord commissioned Elijah for his prophetic assignment, He reminded Elijah of how He set a standard of moral behavior for His people (Mal. 4:4). The Ten Commandments are the moral code of God. Morals are the foundation of the church and democracy. *Moral* means relating to the practice, manners, or conduct of men as social beings, in relation to one another and with reference to right and wrong, general conduct or behavior, especially in sexual matters.

God imparted to Elijah the anointing to change the culture. He set out to change the culture by changing the values. The house of God is where values are changed. This is why Jesus was so furious that He beat the moneychangers out of the temple. Whenever you have buying and selling, corruption is usually around.

The Elijah anointing turns hearts back to God. It challenges the people with the ultimate question: How much longer will you falter between two opinions? (1 Kings 18:21).

The Elijah anointing will offend. God will offend the mind to reveal the heart. God will offend the flesh to reveal the best of your spirit. The Elijah anointing offends natural thinking with the underlying premise to get you pressing into the heart of God. Conflict and tension produce desperation to seek after the Lord.

The primary work of the Elijah prophet is to bring revelation of God's character that shatters the stronghold of hardness of heart that locks the heart away from righteousness.

The Characteristics of an Elijah Prophet

Elijah prophets are preachers of righteousness.

When you, as a prophet, become in the flesh what your generation needs, they will despise you. The question becomes, "Who do you think you are?"

Elijah prophets stand against churches of compromise and temples of tolerance.

Although there are many prophets in the Bible, Elijah stands out as being a symbol of the prophets. Elijah suddenly appears on the scene during a time of great apostasy in Israel. Ahab marries Jezebel and takes Israel to a level of wickedness through the worship of Baal.

> In the tradition of Samuel, Elijah was the head of the school of prophets. Under him were the sons of the prophets—literally hundreds of seers and prophetic minstrels—who proclaimed the Word of the Lord. In this war, however, Jezebel had viciously and systematically murdered all of God's servants until only Elijah remained (see 1 Kings 18:22). Elijah, as the last of the prophets, then challenged the 450 prophets of Baal and the 400 prophets of the Asherah to a demonstration of power: their gods against the power of the Lord.[2]

This provides the background for Elijah's opposition to Ahab and Jezebel. Elijah was fighting for his life and the lives of the prophets. The prophetic ministry in Israel was on the verge of being wiped out. What began to be developed during the time of Samuel was threatened, and Elijah stood up against this murderous system and pronounced judgment upon it.

This backdrop reveals the courage and boldness of Elijah. His ministry was the last bulwark against Jezebel, the false prophets, and Baal. He confronted this with power and authority. He was fighting for a nation that had been seduced by Jezebel and the spirit of idolatry. It was truly a dire situation.

Elijah is called a man of "like passions." In other words, he was a "man" anointed by the Spirit of God. This shows the power of a prophetic mantle.

> And it came to pass, when Joram saw Jehu, that he said, Is it peace, Jehu? And he answered, What peace, so long as the

whoredoms of thy mother Jezebel and her witchcrafts are so
many?

—2 KINGS 9:22

Elijah was not just confronting a natural enemy but also the
power of witchcraft. Israel was being seduced by the powers of
witchcraft and sorcery. Prophets have an anointing to challenge
and deal with witchcraft and sorcery.

Elijah was sent by God to call Israel back to covenant and turn
their hearts back to God. Elijah stands for uncompromising righteousness. Elijah stands against idolatry and the idols that draw
men away from the true God.

The prophets of God were covenant messengers sent to call Israel
back to covenant and warn them of covenant violations. The kings
of Israel were told to keep a copy of the covenant and read it all
their days. Failure to keep covenant resulted in covenant wrath.
Elijah stands with Moses on the Mount of Transfiguration representing the prophets, while Moses represents the Law.

As I said previously, Elijah prophets stand against churches
of compromise and temples of tolerance. The Elijah anointing
comes against illegal authority. They confront the witchcraft and
whoredom of Jezebel.

Baal worship was a fertility cult that was filled with sexual perversion and licentiousness. Elijah confronted the sexual perversion
and wickedness of this worship. Elijah prophets will stand against
perversion and immorality.

John the Baptist, the greatest of the old covenant prophets, came
in the spirit and power of Elijah (Luke 1:17). He came to turn the
hearts of the fathers to the children and the hearts of the children
to the fathers, lest the land would come under a curse (Mal. 4:6).
The curse was the result of covenant violations.

> And Elijah the Tishbite, who was of the inhabitants of Gilead,
> said unto Ahab, As the LORD God of Israel liveth, before

whom I stand, there shall not be dew nor rain these years, but according to my word.

—1 KINGS 17:1

The prophet Elijah just seems to appear on the scene out of nowhere with a declaration that there would be no rain. He shut up the heavens through his prayers. This is the authority and power of a prophet's prayer. Prophetic praying can even affect the elements.

Elijah was concerned with the worship of the true God. Baal worship was false worship. Prophets are concerned with altars that represent worship. Prophets will confront idolatry and false worship. They have a jealousy for the holiness and majesty of God.

Baal worship was directed to Baal and Asherah, whom the people believed sent rain to bring forth their crops. Elijah's intercession to stop the rain was a direct assault against this principality that had held God's people in bondage and deception. God controlled the rain and prosperity, not Baal.

Prophets will deal with strongholds that have held people, cities, and nations captive for years. Through prayer and the word of the Lord prophets will assault the heart of evil and rip it out.

> And Elijah said unto her, Fear not; go and do as thou hast said: but make me thereof a little cake first, and bring it unto me, and after make for thee and for thy son.... And she went and did according to the saying of Elijah: and she, and he, and her house, did eat many days. And the barrel of meal wasted not, neither did the cruse of oil fail, according to the word of the LORD, which he spake by Elijah.
>
> —1 KINGS 17:13, 15–16

This is a miracle of provision. Prophets can bring help in desperate times and situations. The woman was about to die, and God sent the prophet to her to be sustained. The widow sustained Elijah and also received a miracle for herself in the process.

People who support the prophetic ministry can receive the

blessing of the prophet. This is also known as the prophet's reward. God rewards those who minister to those He sends.

Elijah was sent to a widow of Zarephath. There were many widows in Israel, but Elijah was sent to one outside of Israel. This is because he was not honored in Israel. Prophets should be honored and received.

Mighty in Word and Deed

> And the LORD heard the voice of Elijah; and the soul of the child came into him again, and he revived....And the woman said to Elijah, Now by this I know that thou art a man of God, and that the word of the LORD in thy mouth is truth.
>
> —1 KINGS 17:22–24

Elijah performed miracles. He raised this child from the dead. Prophets can have miracle ministries. We should not limit the prophet's ministry to just prophesying. Prophets can minister healing and deliverance. Elisha also worked miracles. Moses was a prophet who was mighty in miracles—in words and deeds (Acts 7:22).

God confirms His word with signs following. Prophets can demonstrate the power of God. Miracles bring great conviction and deliverance. Prophetic praying can also release miracles. Prophetic preaching can release miracles.

> And he said unto them, What things? And they said unto him, Concerning Jesus of Nazareth, which was a prophet mighty in deed and word before God and all the people.
>
> —LUKE 24:19

Prophets can be mighty in word and deed. The prophetic is also the realm of miracles. Notice the miracles of Elijah and Elisha:

- Widow of Zarephath's meal and oil increased (1 Kings 17:14–16)

- Widow's son raised from the dead (1 Kings 17:17–24)

- Drought at Elijah's prayers (1 Kings 17:1–7)

- Fire at Elijah's prayers (1 Kings 18:19–39)

- Rain at Elijah's prayers (1 Kings 18:41–45)

- Elijah fed by ravens (1 Kings 17: 4, 6)

- Waters of Jericho healed by Elisha's casting salt into them (2 Kings 2:21–22)

- Water provided for Jehoshaphat and the allied army (2 Kings 3:16–20)

- The widow's oil multiplied (2 Kings 4:2–7)

- The Shunammite's son given and raised from the dead at Shunem (2 Kings 4:32–37)

- The deadly pottage cured with meal at Gilgal (2 Kings 4:38–41)

- A hundred men fed with twenty loaves at Gilgal (2 Kings 4:42–44)

- Naaman cured of leprosy; Gehazi afflicted with it (2 Kings 5:10–27)

- The iron axe head made to swim in the river Jordan (2 Kings 6:5–7)

- Ben Hadad's plans discovered; Hazael's thoughts, etc. (2 Kings 6:12; 2 Kings 8:7–15)

- The Syrian army smitten with blindness at Dothan (2 Kings 6:18)

- Elisha's bones revive the dead (2 Kings 13:21)

Prophets can operate in healing, deliverance, and miracles. It is important to note that John the Baptist did not do any miracles, yet he was a prophet. Miracles are displays of God's power that bring conviction and breakthrough. I believe the miracle level of a church can increase with an increase of the prophetic level. God's word is supernatural, and how desperately we need the supernatural in our churches today.

Chapter 15

Breaking the Drought

And it came to pass after many days, that the word of the
LORD came to Elijah in the third year, saying, Go, shew
thyself unto Ahab; and I will send rain upon the earth.

— 1 KINGS 18:1

LIJAH PRAYED AGAIN and caused the heavens to be opened.
He did so by the word of the Lord. This again shows the
power of prophetic intercession and God using men to show
judgment or mercy. Again it was proof that God controlled the
rain, not Baal.

Prophets can break the drought in your life and ministry.
Prophets can release living water to regions and churches. Prophets
can help open a closed heaven. Synonyms for *drought* include
shortage, lack, deficit, deficiency, want, need, shortfall, scarcity,
dearth, and insufficiency.

Prophets and prophetic people can break the power of lack. They
help release water, which represents prosperity.

Drought is the result of rebellion. "The rebellious dwell in a dry
land" (Ps. 68:6). Prophets can challenge the idolatry and rebellion
that bring drought, both natural and spiritual. God does not want
His people living in a dry place. God desires to bless His people
with rain.

Prophets can help discern the reason for drought. They are the
key to breaking drought. There are many regions that are spiritually

dry. There are churches that are spiritually dry. The prophet's ministry is a key to breaking drought.

God promised His people that if they humble themselves, pray, seek His face, and turn from their wicked ways, He would heal the land and send rain (2 Chron. 7:13–14). The prophet can help bring humility and repentance through a convicting word. There was drought during the reign of David because of an injustice.

> And it came to pass, when Ahab saw Elijah, that Ahab said unto him, Art thou he that troubleth Israel?
>
> —1 KINGS 18:17

Prophets are often viewed as troublemakers. Ahab blamed Elijah for the trouble in Israel. Elijah responded by blaming Ahab and Jezebel for Israel's trouble. God used Elijah the prophet to release His judgments upon the nation.

> And Elijah came unto all the people, and said, How long halt ye between two opinions? if the LORD be God, follow him: but if Baal, then follow him. And the people answered him not a word.
>
> —1 KINGS 18:21

Prophets hate double-mindedness. They want to see a commitment. They challenge people to make a decision. They call people to wholehearted obedience to God.

> And it came to pass at noon, that Elijah mocked them, and said, Cry aloud: for he is a god; either he is talking, or he is pursuing, or he is in a journey, or peradventure he sleepeth, and must be awaked.
>
> —1 KINGS 18:27

Elijah mocked the prophets of Baal. He mocked the stupidity of idolatry. He did not fear Baal. He challenged Baal to answer by fire.

Elijah represents the God that answers by fire. This was another challenge to Baal, who was considered the possessor of fire.

Whoever has fire has power. Fire provides warmth. Fire cooks our food. Ancient people worshipped gods of fire. Many worshipped sun gods and goddesses. Fire has always played an important part of daily life. God is the true creator of fire. He provided a pillar of fire to protect His people in the wilderness.

> And call ye on the name of your gods, and I will call on the name of the LORD: and the God that answereth by fire, let him be God. And all the people answered and said, It is well spoken.
>
> —1 KINGS 18:24

The true God answers by fire. Fire represents power, purity, and judgment. "Our God is a consuming fire" (Heb. 12:29). God appeared as fire to Israel on Mt. Sinai. God spoke out of the midst of the fire. This caused the people to fear. The fear of God is needed to properly worship and serve God. Elijah prophets bring back the fear of the Lord.

Fire represents purity, power, holiness, and judgment. The Lord descended upon Sinai in a fire.

> And mount Sinai was altogether on a smoke, because the LORD descended upon it in fire: and the smoke thereof ascended as the smoke of a furnace, and the whole mount quaked greatly.
>
> —EXODUS 19:18

Notice the response of the people:

> And all the people saw the thunderings, and the lightnings, and the noise of the trumpet, and the mountain smoking: and when the people saw it, they removed, and stood afar off. And they said unto Moses, Speak thou with us, and we will hear: but let not God speak with us, lest we die. And Moses said

> unto the people, Fear not: for God is come to prove you, and
> that his fear may be before your faces, that ye sin not.
>
> —EXODUS 20:18–20

The people feared God when they saw Him come down on Sinai in fire. Elijah prophets bring back the fear of God. They represent the God who answers by fire. They call us back to covenant. Fire represents the judgment upon broken covenant. John who came in the power and spirit of Elijah warned Israel about a coming baptism of fire (Matt. 3:11). He called upon them to repent. Many responded and returned to the fear of God.

> And Elijah said unto them, Take the prophets of Baal; let not
> one of them escape. And they took them: and Elijah brought
> them down to the brook Kishon, and slew them there.
>
> —1 KINGS 18:40

Elijah executed the prophets of Baal. This was not the action of a timid man. This was the action of someone who feared God and was faithful to the covenant. The covenant demanded death to those who led Israel astray. Elijah was simply executing the laws of the covenant.

Elijah stands against false prophetic ministries. Elijah confronted the prophets who were at Jezebel's table. His execution of the prophets was an attack on Jezebel. Prophets deal with the powers of darkness, especially Jezebel spirits of idolatry and witchcraft. Elijah prophesied judgment upon Jezebel that was eventually executed by Jehu.

Elijah spoke Jezebel's judgment over the incident of Naboth and his vineyard (1 Kings 21). He spoke against the injustice of Ahab and Jezebel. Prophets hate injustice because God hates injustice. In other words prophets hate what God hates.

And it came to pass, when Ahab heard those words, that he
rent his clothes, and put sackcloth upon his flesh, and fasted,
and lay in sackcloth, and went softly.

—1 KINGS 21:27

Ahab was convicted by the words of Elijah. Ahab humbled himself, and God responded by promising him that judgment would
not come in his lifetime. God is a God of mercy, and repentance
will move His heart. There is no record that Jezebel ever humbled
herself.

The prophetic word can bring conviction. The prophetic word
will challenge sin and rebellion. The prophetic word does not
respect persons. Elijah confronted Ahab, even though he was the
king. Elijah held Ahab responsible for the sin of Israel. Leaders have
a higher responsibility to live according to God's standards.

And Elijah said unto Ahab, Get thee up, eat and drink; for
there is a sound of abundance of rain.

—1 KINGS 18:41

Elijah closed heaven with his prayers, and at the word of the Lord
he prayed for heaven to be opened. Prophets can tell when there is
an abundance of rain on the horizon. Rain represents mercy and
blessing. Prophetic praying can open the heavens and cause the
rain to fall.

Rain comes to break drought. Drought represents the curse. Dry
places need the rain of God. Repentance is necessary for the rain to
come. Churches desperately need an abundance of rain.

So Ahab went up to eat and to drink. And Elijah went up to
the top of Carmel; and he cast himself down upon the earth,
and put his face between his knees,

—1 KINGS 18:42

Elijah did not only declare the rain was coming, but he also
prayed for the rain. This is an important aspect of the prophet's

ministry. Prophets pray over what they see. They can birth the revelation given to them by God. The cloud formed as a result of Elijah's prayer. Prophetic intercession is a powerful way to see the release of the word of the Lord.

> And the hand of the LORD was on Elijah; and he girded up his loins, and ran before Ahab to the entrance of Jezreel.
> —1 KINGS 18:46

> And Ahab told Jezebel all that Elijah had done, and withal how he had slain all the prophets with the sword. Then Jezebel sent a messenger unto Elijah, saying, So let the gods do to me, and more also, if I make not thy life as the life of one of them by to morrow about this time.
> —1 KINGS 19:1–2

Jezebel hated the true prophets of God. She was a witch and a high priestess of Baal. She was a demonized woman who was filled with demons of witchcraft, idolatry, rebellion, and murder. She was ruthless in her hatred of the true God and His messengers.

This was not an empty threat. Jezebel had already killed the prophets of God and was intending to kill Elijah. Elijah knew what he was dealing with. Elijah was threatened by a witch who was ruthless and intimidating. She was demonized.

Elijah prophets deal with the demonization of society. Idol worship was demon worship (Lev. 17:7; Deut. 32:17). The pagans sacrificed to demons and not to God. If there is no prophetic, there is no stop to the process of demonization. Even the people of God were being demonized by the idolatry of Jezebel.

Children are sacrificed on the altar of demons (Ps. 106:37). The entire family is affected. Society begins to break down with immorality. The family unit ends up being destroyed. Prophets are a bulwark against the flood of evil and wickedness.

Prophets Are Human

And he came thither unto a cave, and lodged there; and,
behold, the word of the LORD came to him, and he said unto
him, What doest thou here, Elijah?

—1 KINGS 19:9

Elijah ran from the threat of Jezebel. He was probably exhausted
from the encounter on Mt. Carmel and the killing of the prophets
of Baal. This shows the human side of the prophets. Elijah felt all
alone and complained to God that he was the only one left. God
reminded him that there were seven thousand in Israel who were
faithful to covenant.

Prophets are human and also need encouragement. Elijah
ran from Jezebel. He feared for his life. Jezebel was the killer of
prophets. Demons hate prophets. Jezebel was a witch who used fear
and intimidation to control the nation.

Prophets are human and are subject to the same passions as
all men. Prophets must operate by the strength of God, but they
also need encouragement and prayer. Prophets can also be blessed
by receiving the prophetic word. Prophets should not be exalted
beyond measure.

Elias was a man subject to like passions as we are, and he
prayed earnestly that it might not rain: and it rained not on
the earth by the space of three years and six months.

—JAMES 5:17

Prophets May Show Up Out of Nowhere to Break a Drought

And now thou sayest, Go, tell thy lord, Behold, Elijah is here.
And it shall come to pass, as soon as I am gone from thee, that
the Spirit of the LORD shall carry thee whither I know not;

and so when I come and tell Ahab, and he cannot find thee, he
shall slay me: but I thy servant fear the LORD from my youth.

—1 KINGS 18:11–12

Some believe that the Spirit carried Elijah to different places. Others
believe that Obadiah said this because Elijah had disappeared for
three years after announcing a drought and had not been seen.
Elijah tends to show up suddenly out of nowhere to announce the
word of the Lord. Obadiah was afraid to tell Ahab that Elijah was
there only for him to disappear again.

Don't be surprised if prophets show up out of nowhere with the
word of the Lord. Many are now in the desert places hidden by God.
They appear when the time is right. They appear with the word
of the Lord. God hid Elijah from the wrath of Jezebel, who had
killed the prophets of the Lord. God never leaves Himself without
a witness.

So he departed thence, and found Elisha the son of Shaphat,
who was plowing with twelve yoke of oxen before him, and
he with the twelfth: and Elijah passed by him, and cast his
mantle upon him.

—1 KINGS 19:19

Elijah was told to anoint Elisha to be a prophet in his place.
God was about to take Elijah to heaven. Elijah's mantle came upon
Elisha, who received a double portion of his spirit.

God uses prophets to impart to emerging prophets. The mantle
represented the anointing of the prophet. Elisha would be trained
by Elijah and receive a double portion of his spirit.

God selected Elisha, not Elijah. God calls prophets, not man.
Elisha would fill the vacancy after Elijah's departure. Impartation
is one of the main functions of a prophet. To impart means to
transfer. The anointing is transferable.

> And Ahab said to Elijah, Hast thou found me, O mine enemy? And he answered, I have found thee: because thou hast sold thyself to work evil in the sight of the LORD.
>
> —1 KINGS 21:20

Elijah was Ahab's enemy. Prophets are the enemies of the ungodly. They are the enemy of the enemies of God. An enemy is a person who is actively opposed or hostile to someone or something. Elijah was opposed to the idolatry and wickedness of Ahab. Ahab and Jezebel had become the enemies of God.

The Garments of a Prophet

> And they answered him, He was an hairy man, and girt with a girdle of leather about his loins. And he said, It is Elijah the Tishbite.
>
> —2 KINGS 1:8

Elijah's garment identified him. Elijah's clothing represented the roughness of his anointing. He was not a man of soft clothing. Jesus said men with soft raiment lived in kings' houses (Matt. 11:8). Sometimes prophets are told to be soft. Elijah did not have soft words for Israel. Elijah was not a soft man. Elijah and John were wilderness prophets.

There are many today who only want soft words. They don't want anyone with a mantle like Elijah. Elijahs have to sometimes speak hard words.

> And it came to pass, when the LORD would take up Elijah into heaven by a whirlwind, that Elijah went with Elisha from Gilgal.
>
> —2 KINGS 2:1

Elijah was taken to heaven in a whirlwind.

> And Elijah took his mantle, and wrapped it together, and
> smote the waters, and they were divided hither and thither, so
> that they two went over on dry ground.
>
> —2 KINGS 2:8

This is the mantle of the prophet. The mantle was the official garment of a prophet. Throwing it over the shoulders of Elisha was a
symbolic act denoting his summons to the office of prophet, but it
was also a sure sign of God's gift that enabled him to fulfill the prophetic office and ministry.

Notice the supernatural aspects of Elijah's ministry:

> And it came to pass, as they still went on, and talked, that,
> behold, there appeared a chariot of fire, and horses of fire, and
> parted them both asunder; and Elijah went up by a whirlwind
> into heaven.
>
> —2 KINGS 2:11

> And he took the mantle of Elijah that fell from him, and
> smote the waters, and said, Where is the LORD God of Elijah?
> and when he also had smitten the waters, they parted hither
> and thither: and Elisha went over.
>
> —2 KINGS 2:14

> Wherefore they came again, and told him. And he said, This
> is the word of the LORD, which he spake by his servant Elijah
> the Tishbite, saying, In the portion of Jezreel shall dogs eat the
> flesh of Jezebel.
>
> —2 KINGS 9:36

Regardless of Elijah's great power, the lack of faith in Israel pre-
vented many from receiving miracles. The prophet's ministry will
flourish in an atmosphere of faith. Even Christ, the greatest prophet,
could do no mighty works in His hometown because of unbelief.

> But I tell you of a truth, many widows were in Israel in the
> days of Elias, when the heaven was shut up three years and six

months, when great famine was throughout all the land; but unto none of them was Elias sent, save unto Sarepta, a city of Sidon, unto a woman that was a widow.

—LUKE 4:25–26

Chapter 16

One Hundred Advantages of the Word of the Lord

Bless the LORD, *O my soul, and forget not all his benefits.*

—PSALM 103:2

THE WORD OF the Lord releases great benefits to the believer. Understanding these benefits will give us a greater desire to operate in a greater level of prophecy. Benefit is an advantage. This again is the prophetic advantage.

1. The prophetic word brings healing and deliverance.

He sent his word, and healed them, and delivered them from their destructions.

—PSALM 107:20

I have seen many believers healed and delivered through the prophetic word. Prophecy is a powerful tool that releases miracles. The word of the Lord carries the anointing and virtue of God that brings healing and deliverance to the recipient.

2. The prophetic word resurrects (Ezek. 37).

When Ezekiel prophesied, the dead bones came to life. Prophecy has resurrection power. God's word is full of life. I have seen prophecy resurrect visions and dreams that have died. I have seen believers "come alive" when receiving prophecy.

3. The prophetic word is a lamp and a light.

> Thy word is a lamp unto my feet, and a light unto my path.
>
> —Psalm 119:105

Every believer needs a lamp and a light helping them see their way. The prophetic word can illuminate the darkness and cause believers to see where they are going. Prophecy shines on our paths and makes it easier to see where we are going.

4. The prophetic word edifies, exhorts, and comforts (1 Cor. 14).

To edify means to build. It is the root of the word *edifice* (a building). The prophetic word builds up the believer and builds up the church. To exhort means to encourage. Every believer needs encouragement. *Comfort* means to give strength and hope, to cheer.

5. The prophetic word falls like rain (Deut. 32:2).

The prophetic word refreshes. Rain is needed to bring forth a harvest. Every believer needs the rain of the Spirit to fall. Rain symbolizes the blessing of heaven. Prophecy is the word coming from heaven that falls upon our lives.

6. The prophetic word roots out, tears down, pulls down, destroys, builds, and plants (Jer. 1:10).

Prophecy roots out the things that have been planted by the enemy. Prophecy tears down the strongholds that have been built by the enemy. Prophecy pulls down the high things of the enemy. Prophecy destroys the works of the devil. Prophecy also builds and plants. Things must be rooted out, pulled down, torn down, and destroyed before we can build and plant.

7. The prophetic word is a light that shines in a dark place.

> We have also a more sure word of prophecy; whereunto ye
> do well that ye take heed, as unto a light that shineth in a
> dark place, until the day dawn, and the day star arise in your
> hearts.
>
> —2 PETER 1:19

Many believers find themselves in a dark place. They have no
light or illumination concerning the will of God or what they are
experiencing. Prophecy is a light that shines in our dark places.
Prophecy helps us overcome any darkness or blind spots that we
are experiencing.

8. The prophetic word causes the winds to blow (Ezek. 37).

Ezekiel prophesied to the winds. The winds represent the breath
of God. Winds are needed to bring change and refreshing. There
are many different kinds of winds. The winds of refreshing and life
need to blow in our lives. Old things need to be blown away, and
new things need to be blown in.

9. The prophetic word can change you into another man (1 Sam. 10).

Saul was turned into another man when he came into contact
with the company of prophets. Saul was changed and began to
prophesy. I have seen people change as a result of prophecy. Many
have said what they experienced was life changing.

10. The prophetic word is like a fire and a hammer.

> Is not my word like as a fire? saith the LORD; and like a
> hammer that breaketh the rock in pieces?
>
> —JEREMIAH 23:29

Fire burns and hammers break. The word of the Lord can burn things out of your life. The prophetic word is like a hammer that breaks the rock. Hard things are demolished through the prophetic word.

11. The prophetic word reveals the secrets of the heart.

> And thus are the secrets of his heart made manifest…
>
> —1 CORINTHIANS 14:25

God knows the heart and uses the prophetic word to reveal the secrets of the heart. People who experience prophecy know it could only be God who revealed what was in their heart. Prophecy is a powerful sign that God knows and understands what we are thinking.

12. The prophetic word provokes worship.

> …and so falling down on his face he will worship God, and report that God is in you of a truth.
>
> —1 CORINTHIANS 14:25

Prophecy can stir men to worship and acknowledge the omniscient God. God knows all and causes wonder and amazement when He speaks only what we know in our hearts. I have seen many fall down and bow as a result of prophecy.

13. Gifts can be imparted through the prophetic word.

> Neglect not the gift that is in thee, which was given thee by prophecy, with the laying on of the hands of the presbytery.
>
> —1 TIMOTHY 4:14

Prophetic presbytery is an important function in imparting gifts into the life of the recipient.

14. The prophetic word blesses.

> And this is the blessing, wherewith Moses the man of God blessed the children of Israel before his death.
>
> —DEUTERONOMY 33:1

Moses blessed the tribes of Israel through prophecy. To bless means to confer well-being or prosperity on. The word of the Lord can release tremendous blessings upon the recipient. Moses blessed them and spoke concerning their future. Prophetic blessing helps release us into our destinies with the favor of God.

15. The prophetic word can come in a vision.

> After these things the word of the LORD came unto Abram in a vision, saying, Fear not, Abram: I am thy shield, and thy exceeding great reward.
>
> —GENESIS 15:1

God revealed His word to Abraham in a vision. The prophetic word is not limited to what we speak but can come through what we see in a vision or a dream.

16. The prophetic word releases signs and judgments.

> The altar also was rent, and the ashes poured out from the altar, according to the sign which the man of God had given by the word of the LORD.
>
> —1 KINGS 13:5

The prophetic word can bring judgment. Judgments are a sign of the power and righteousness of God.

17. Through the prophetic word the Lord reveals Himself.

> And the LORD appeared again in Shiloh: for the LORD revealed himself to Samuel in Shiloh by the word of the LORD.
>
> —1 SAMUEL 3:21

The Lord reveals Himself through prophecy. He reveals His character, love, power, righteousness, wisdom, compassion, mercy, and judgment through prophecy. Those who prophesy will have a greater revelation of the God who speaks.

18. The prophetic word gives revelation of God's purpose for your life.

> Where there is no revelation [or prophetic vision], the people cast off restraint; but happy is he who keeps the law.
>
> —PROVERBS 29:18, NKJV

19. The Holy Spirit puts the prophetic word in your tongue.

> The Spirit of the LORD spake by me, and his word was in my tongue.
>
> —2 SAMUEL 23:2

We prophesy by the Holy Spirit. The Holy Spirit puts the words of God in our tongue (mouth, lips), and we simply release it.

20. The prophetic word allows us to see God.

> And he said, Hear thou therefore the word of the LORD: I saw the LORD sitting on his throne, and all the host of heaven standing by him on his right hand and on his left.
>
> —1 KINGS 22:19

Sometimes the word of the Lord is delivered by what we see. Some prophesy by the *nabi* flow (bubbling up), and some prophesy with a visionary flow (what they see). We can also have a combination of both.

21. The prophetic allows us to inquire of the Lord.

> And Jehoshaphat said unto the king of Israel, Enquire, I pray thee, at the word of the LORD to day.
>
> —1 KINGS 22:5

It was a common practice to inquire of the Lord through prophets. We can ask for prophetic direction and insight from those who prophesy.

22. The word of the Lord changes things quickly.

> Then Elisha said, Hear ye the word of the LORD; Thus saith the LORD, To morrow about this time shall a measure of fine flour be sold for a shekel, and two measures of barley for a shekel, in the gate of Samaria.
>
> —2 KINGS 7:1

I have seen miracle turnarounds in the lives of those who receive prophecy. The prophetic word can change a person's finances, marriage, family, ministry, and so on. There is nothing impossible with God.

23. The word of the Lord destroys Jezebel.

> Wherefore they came again, and told him. And he said, This is the word of the LORD, which he spake by his servant Elijah the Tishbite, saying, In the portion of Jezreel shall dogs eat the flesh of Jezebel.
>
> —2 KINGS 9:36

Judgment came upon Jezebel after Elijah delivered the word of the Lord. The word of the Lord can bring judgment, and there were few people more wicked than Jezebel. The spirit of Jezebel hates the true prophetic anointing and will attack it viciously. The prophetic is a weapon against Jezebel spirits and helps defeat this evil entity.

24. The word of the Lord brings restoration.

> He restored the coast of Israel from the entering of Hamath unto the sea of the plain, according to the word of the LORD God of Israel, which he spake by the hand of his servant Jonah, the son of Amittai, the prophet, which was of Gathhepher.
>
> —2 KINGS 14:25

There are multitudes of people who need restoration in their marriages, finances, and ministries. The word of the Lord is a powerful way to bring restoration.

25. The word of the Lord can bring evil upon a place.

> Thus saith the LORD, Behold, I will bring evil upon this place, and upon the inhabitants thereof, even all the words of the book which the king of Judah hath read.
>
> —2 KINGS 22:16

God rewards wickedness with evil. God allows evil to come upon a place for disobedience and rebellion. The word of the Lord releases judgment and cleanses wickedness from the land.

26. The word of the Lord comes to those who humble themselves.

> And when the LORD saw that they humbled themselves, the word of the LORD came to Shemaiah, saying, They have humbled themselves; therefore I will not destroy them, but I will

grant them some deliverance; and my wrath shall not be poured out upon Jerusalem by the hand of Shishak.

—2 CHRONICLES 12:7

God gives grace to the humble. Humility always attracts the blessing of the Lord. Grace is released through prophecy. Humility brings deliverance. The prophetic word also brings deliverance.

27. The word of the Lord releases wrath upon those who despise it.

But they mocked the messengers of God, and despised his words, and misused his prophets, until the wrath of the LORD arose against his people, till there was no remedy.

—2 CHRONICLES 36:16

It is dangerous to despise prophecy. Prophecy often brings warning, and those who despise it do so at their own peril.

28. The word of the Lord stirs the spirits of kings.

Now in the first year of Cyrus king of Persia, that the word of the LORD spoken by the mouth of Jeremiah might be accomplished, the LORD stirred up the spirit of Cyrus king of Persia, that he made a proclamation throughout all his kingdom, and put it also in writing.

—2 CHRONICLES 36:22

Jeremiah prophesied a seventy-year captivity in Babylon. After the seventy years the Lord stirred the spirit of Cyrus to issue a decree for the rebuilding of the temple.

29. The word of the Lord is pure.

> The words of the LORD are pure words: as silver tried in a furnace of earth, purified seven times.
>
> —PSALM 12:6

True prophecy is pure. Those who corrupt the word of the Lord are often false prophets or those with hidden agendas. Those who prophesy must have pure motives. Prophecy should be done in love and sincerity.

30. The word of the Lord is right.

> For the word of the LORD is right; and all his works are done in truth.
>
> —PSALM 33:4

Right means morally good or acceptable. We must speak right things and avoid speaking that which is corrupt or unclean.

31. The word of the Lord causes praise.

> In God will I praise his word: in the LORD will I praise his word.
>
> —PSALM 56:10

Prophecy releases praise. Churches that operate in the prophetic will have a high level of praise.

32. The word of the Lord will test you.

> Until the time that his word came: the word of the LORD tried him.
>
> —PSALM 105:19

The word of the Lord sometimes requires patience before fulfillment. The word will test your obedience and love for the Lord.

33. The word of the Lord will quicken you.

I am afflicted very much: quicken me, O LORD, according unto thy word.

—PSALM 119:107

To quicken means to make alive. *Quicken* means to give life. This is much needed, especially for those in affliction.

34. The word of the Lord gives hope.

I wait for the LORD, my soul doth wait, and in his word do I hope.

—PSALM 130:5

Hope is the anchor of the soul. Without hope our lives are anchorless, and we drift. Hopelessness causes discouragement and despair. Prophecy restores hope and brings encouragement.

35. The word of the Lord gives understanding.

Let my cry come near before thee, O LORD: give me understanding according to thy word.

—PSALM 119:169

Prophecy helps us understand the will of God. Prophecy also gives us a better understanding of what we are dealing with in life. Life can be perplexing, and there are many who end up confused. Prophecy gives us answers and helps us live our lives with confidence and assurance.

36. The word of the Lord empties and spoils.

> The land shall be utterly emptied, and utterly spoiled: for the
> LORD hath spoken this word.
>
> —ISAIAH 24:3

The prophetic word can release judgments upon wickedness and
rebellion.

37. The word of the Lord brings trembling.

> For all those things hath mine hand made, and all those
> things have been, saith the LORD: but to this man will I look,
> even to him that is poor and of a contrite spirit, and trembleth
> at my word.
>
> —ISAIAH 66:2

Prophecy releases the fear of the Lord. We desperately need the
reverential fear of the Lord to walk properly and to please God.

38. The word of the Lord comes in famine.

> The word of the LORD that came to Jeremiah concerning the
> dearth.
>
> —JEREMIAH 14:1

Prophecy can give us the reason why we are experiencing famine,
and prophecy can help break the famine.

39. The earth (land) hears the word of the Lord.

> O earth, earth, earth, hear the word of the LORD.
>
> —JEREMIAH 22:29

This also includes man who was taken from the earth. The land
is very important to God and His purposes.

40. The word of the Lord comes from those who stand in the counsel of the Lord.

For who hath stood in the counsel of the LORD, and hath perceived and heard his word? who hath marked his word, and heard it?

—JEREMIAH 23:18

Prophets stand in the counsel of the Lord. They have insight into the plans and purposes of God for individuals, churches, and nations.

41. The prophetic word gives courage.

And when Asa heard these words, and the prophecy of Oded the prophet, he took courage, and put away the abominable idols out of all the land of Judah and Benjamin, and out of the cities which he had taken from mount Ephraim, and renewed the altar of the LORD, that was before the porch of the LORD.

—2 CHRONICLES 15:8

We need courage to deal with life's challenges. Asa received the courage he needed to carry out the reforms needed in Israel. Asa received courage and was able to overcome any hesitancy in carrying out the needed reforms.

42. The prophetic word delivered in love means everything.

And though I have the gift of prophecy, and understand all mysteries, and all knowledge; and though I have all faith, so that I could remove mountains, and have not charity, I am nothing.

—1 CORINTHIANS 13:2

Prophets and prophetic people must operate in a high degree of love. Prophetic people who become bitter, angry, and harsh will release tainted words.

43. The prophetic word can be elevated by musical instruments.

Moreover David and the captains of the host separated to the service of the sons of Asaph, and of Heman, and of Jeduthun, who should prophesy with harps, with psalteries, and with cymbals.

—1 CHRONICLES 25:1

Music is an important aspect of the prophetic ministry. There are many musical prophets who have the anointing to prophesy on the instruments.

44. Prophets can help us prosper in building.

And the elders of the Jews builded, and they prospered through the prophesying of Haggai the prophet and Zechariah the son of Iddo. And they builded, and finished it, according to the commandment of the God of Israel, and according to the commandment of Cyrus, and Darius, and Artaxerxes king of Persia.

—EZRA 6:14

The Jews prospered in rebuilding the temple through the help of the prophets Haggai and Zechariah. Prophets help us prosper in the work of the Lord.

45. The word of the Lord compels us to prophesy.

The lion hath roared, who will not fear? the Lord GOD hath spoken, who can but prophesy?

—AMOS 3:8

Those who receive the word must release it. The prophet is moved by God to declare what he or she hears from the Lord.

46. The prophetic word of the Lord encourages team ministry.

> For we know in part, and we prophesy in part.
>
> —1 Corinthians 13:9

We can only speak the part that God gives us to speak. Team ministry is important because each prophetic minister has a part to release.

47. The word of the Lord makes us desire to prophesy.

> Follow after charity, and desire spiritual gifts, but rather that ye may prophesy.
>
> —1 Corinthians 14:1

Desire is an important part of walking stronger in the prophetic. Teaching and preaching on prophecy will increase the desire in the church to operate in the prophetic.

48. The prophetic word teaches and comforts.

> For ye may all prophesy one by one, that all may learn, and all may be comforted.
>
> —1 Corinthians 14:31

Prophecy can bring instruction and great comfort to the recipient.

49. The word of the Lord makes us want to prophesy more.

> Wherefore, brethren, covet to prophesy, and forbid not to speak with tongues.
>
> —1 Corinthians 14:39

Covet is a strong word. *Covet* means to desire strongly. Where there is no desire, there will be a low level of prophecy.

50. The word of the Lord makes us confident in prophecy.

Despise not prophesyings.
—1 THESSALONIANS 5:20

There is a danger of despising prophecy. This can be due to misuse or bad experiences with the prophetic ministry. Some are simply afraid of prophecy.

51. The voice of the Lord comes with His presence.

And they heard the voice of the LORD God walking in the garden in the cool of the day: and Adam and his wife hid themselves from the presence of the LORD God amongst the trees of the garden.
—GENESIS 3:8

Prophecy releases the presence of the Lord. I have seen the atmosphere of church services dramatically change after a strong prophetic utterance.

52. Obeying the voice of the Lord brings health.

And said, If thou wilt diligently hearken to the voice of the LORD thy God, and wilt do that which is right in his sight, and wilt give ear to his commandments, and keep all his statutes, I will put none of these diseases upon thee, which I have brought upon the Egyptians: for I am the LORD that healeth thee.
—EXODUS 15:26

Obeying the prophetic word brings great blessings, including health and prosperity.

53. The voice of the Lord is powerful.

The voice of the Lord is powerful; the voice of the Lord is full of majesty.

—Psalm 29:4

The power of God is released through prophecy. This can include deliverance, healing, and breakthrough. Majesty is royal power.

54. The voice of the Lord breaks the cedars.

The voice of the Lord breaketh the cedars; yea, the Lord breaketh the cedars of Lebanon.

—Psalm 29:5

Cedars are tall and strong trees. This again represents the power of the prophetic word.

55. The voice of the Lord shakes the wilderness.

The voice of the Lord shaketh the wilderness; the Lord shaketh the wilderness of Kadesh.

—Psalm 29:8

Many people have been shaken out of wilderness and dry places through prophecy.

56. The prophetic word confirms.

And Judas and Silas, being prophets also themselves, exhorted the brethren with many words, and confirmed them.

—Acts 15:32

We all need confirmation concerning our callings, gifts, and destiny. The prophetic word confirms believers and gives them strength.

57. The word of the Lord causes us to excel in prophecy.

Even so ye, forasmuch as ye are zealous of spiritual gifts, seek that ye may excel to the edifying of the church.

—1 CORINTHIANS 14:12

We should excel in prophecy. *Excel* means to abound.

58. The word of the Lord makes our proportion of faith grow.

Having then gifts differing according to the grace that is given to us, whether prophecy, let us prophesy according to the proportion of faith.

—ROMANS 12:6

Faith is essential to prophecy. The more you operate in the prophetic, the more your faith will develop in this area.

59. The rebellious can be hewed by the prophets.

Therefore have I hewed them by the prophets; I have slain them by the words of my mouth: and thy judgments are as the light that goeth forth.

—HOSEA 6:5

God used the prophets to hew Israel. To hew means to chop or cut. This is another aspect of the power of prophecy to release judgment.

60. All God's people can be prophetic.

> And Moses said unto him, Enviest thou for my sake? would God that all the Lord's people were prophets, and that the Lord would put his spirit upon them!
>
> —Numbers 11:29

Moses reveals the heart of a leader who desires to see the entire church operate to some degree in the prophetic. I believe this should be the heart and attitude of every leader.

61. We prosper by believing God's prophets.

> And they rose early in the morning, and went forth into the wilderness of Tekoa: and as they went forth, Jehoshaphat stood and said, Hear me, O Judah, and ye inhabitants of Jerusalem; Believe in the Lord your God, so shall ye be established; believe his prophets, so shall ye prosper.
>
> —2 Chronicles 20:20

Prophets have an anointing to break lack and release prosperity. We benefit when we believe the prophets of God. Prophets are sent to be a blessing to us.

62. The prophetic establishes worship.

> And he set the Levites in the house of the Lord with cymbals, with psalteries, and with harps, according to the commandment of David, and of Gad the king's seer, and Nathan the prophet: for so was the commandment of the Lord by his prophets.
>
> —2 Chronicles 29:25

Worship is important to prophets. Prophets rebuked Israel for vain and false worship. The prophetic ministry will enhance true worship.

63. The prophetic word helps us.

> Then rose up Zerubbabel the son of Shealtiel, and Jeshua the son of Jozadak, and began to build the house of God which is at Jerusalem: and with them were the prophets of God helping them.
>
> —EZRA 5:2

Prophets bring great help and assistance to leaders. God used Haggai and Zechariah to encourage Joshua and Zerubbabel, the leaders who were restoring the temple.

64. The prophets of God are protected.

> Saying, Touch not mine anointed, and do my prophets no harm.
>
> —PSALM 105:15

God is jealous over His prophets. God protects, defends, and avenges His sent ones.

65. The prophetic word brings correction and speaks right things.

> Which say to the seers, See not; and to the prophets, Prophesy not unto us right things, speak unto us smooth things, prophesy deceits.
>
> —ISAIAH 30:10

Sometimes the word of the Lord is corrective. The prophetic word can also bring rebuke, and sometimes appear to be hard.

66. The prophetic word reveals secrets.

> Surely the Lord GOD will do nothing, but he revealeth his secret unto his servants the prophets.
>
> —AMOS 3:7

Prophets and prophetic people have revelation of the secrets of God. This shows the importance of prophets in the plan of God.

67. The prophetic word of the Lord causes us to know the deep, hidden things of God.

> But as it is written, Eye hath not seen, nor ear heard, neither have entered into the heart of man, the things which God hath prepared for them that love him. But God hath revealed them unto us by his Spirit: for the Spirit searcheth all things, yea, the deep things of God.
>
> —1 CORINTHIANS 2:9–10

68. The prophetic word causes a noise and a shaking.

> So I prophesied as I was commanded: and as I prophesied, there was a noise, and behold a shaking, and the bones came together, bone to his bone.
>
> —EZEKIEL 37:7

Prophecy shakes things up and causes thing to move in our lives. Nations, churches, and individuals can be shaken by the word. Prophecy can cause things that are disjointed to come together in your life.

69. The prophetic word causes breath to come back.

> So I prophesied as he commanded me, and the breath came into them, and they lived, and stood up upon their feet, an exceeding great army.
>
> —Ezekiel 37:10

Breath is spirit and life. Prophecy restores breath and life to those who are weary and without strength. We need breath and spirit to live.

70. The baptism of the Holy Spirit releases prophecy.

> And when Paul had laid his hands upon them, the Holy Ghost came on them; and they spake with tongues, and prophesied.
>
> —Acts 19:6

The baptism of the Holy Spirit is the doorway to the prophetic realm. Those who receive the Holy Spirit can operate in the prophetic to some degree. Do not limit the baptism of the Holy Spirit to tongues, but include the blessing of prophecy.

71. The word of the Lord causes us to hear.

> Therefore Eli said unto Samuel, Go, lie down: and it shall be, if he call thee, that thou shalt say, Speak, Lord; for thy servant heareth. So Samuel went and lay down in his place.
>
> —1 Samuel 3:9

We should all be open to hear the Lord's voice and release what He gives us. Samuel was young and did not recognize the voice of the Lord. Young prophets need mature prophets to help them learn the ways of the prophetic.

72. The word of the Lord causes us to speak what the Lord commands.

But Balaam answered and said unto Balak, Told not I thee, saying, All that the LORD speaketh, that I must do?

—NUMBERS 23:26

We can only speak what the Lord commands. To speak outside of His command is to operate in presumption.

73. The prophetic word reveals that God is always speaking, yet many don't perceive.

For God speaketh once, yea twice, yet man perceiveth it not.

—JOB 33:14

God is always speaking, yet hardness of heart causes men not to perceive what He is saying.

74. The prophetic word can be like wine ready to burst.

Behold, my belly is as wine which hath no vent; it is ready to burst like new bottles.

—JOB 32:19

Prophets who carry the word must release it. Those who have no outlet often become frustrated.

75. The prophetic word delivers the people from slavery.

And afterward Moses and Aaron went in, and told Pharaoh, Thus saith the LORD God of Israel, Let my people go, that they may hold a feast unto me in the wilderness.

—EXODUS 5:1

The prophetic word breaks bondages and liberates. The prophetic word brings deliverance. God used a prophet to bring Israel out of bondage.

76. The prophetic word breaks barrenness.

> And he went forth unto the spring of the waters, and cast the salt in there, and said, Thus saith the Lord, I have healed these waters; there shall not be from thence any more death or barren land.
>
> —2 Kings 2:21

Fruitfulness is the result of the prophet's ministry. Prophets can identify the cause of barrenness and break lack through the prophetic word.

77. The prophetic word identifies God's anointed.

> And he arose, and went into the house; and he poured the oil on his head, and said unto him, Thus saith the Lord God of Israel, I have anointed thee king over the people of the Lord, even over Israel.
>
> —2 Kings 9:6

Prophets are used by God to identify leaders. Churches need prophets to help identify emerging leaders and impart into their lives. God used Samuel to identify Saul and David as the first kings of Israel.

78. The prophetic word releases healing.

> Turn again, and tell Hezekiah the captain of my people, Thus saith the Lord, the God of David thy father, I have heard thy

prayer, I have seen thy tears: behold, I will heal thee: on the third day thou shalt go up unto the house of the LORD.

—2 KINGS 20:5

Prophets can also be used in the healing ministry. The prophetic word can release healing. Prophets can reveal the will of God to heal as answer to prayer.

79. The prophetic word drives out fear.

And he said, Hearken ye, all Judah, and ye inhabitants of Jerusalem, and thou king Jehoshaphat, Thus saith the LORD unto you, Be not afraid nor dismayed by reason of this great multitude; for the battle is not yours, but God's.

—2 CHRONICLES 20:15

Fear is one of the greatest enemies of progress. Prophecy can release boldness and courage to overcome fear and hesitance. Prophecy encourages us that God is on our side.

80. The prophetic word stops the plans of the enemy.

Thus saith the Lord GOD, It shall not stand, neither shall it come to pass.

—ISAIAH 7:7

Prophecy is a weapon against the plans of hell. The plans of hell are brought to nothing through prophetic intercession and declaration.

81. The prophetic word establishes foundation.

Therefore thus saith the Lord GOD, Behold, I lay in Zion for a foundation a stone, a tried stone, a precious corner stone, a sure foundation: he that believeth shall not make haste.

—ISAIAH 28:16

A strong foundation is important to build upon. Prophecy speaks to the foundational issues of our life.

82. The prophetic word makes a path.

> Thus saith the LORD, which maketh a way in the sea, and a path in the mighty waters.
> —ISAIAH 43:16

Prophecy opens the way for us to prosper. God opens doors and establishes our path through the prophetic ministry.

83. The prophetic word teaches us to profit.

> Thus saith the LORD, thy Redeemer, the Holy One of Israel; I am the LORD thy God which teacheth thee to profit, which leadeth thee by the way that thou shouldest go.
> —ISAIAH 48:17

This is another aspect of prosperity. Prophecy helps direct our way so that we can prosper. Prophecy encourages us to prosper.

84. The prophetic word releases peace.

> For thus saith the LORD, Behold, I will extend peace to her like a river, and the glory of the Gentiles like a flowing stream: then shall ye suck, ye shall be borne upon her sides, and be dandled upon her knees.
> —ISAIAH 66:12

Peace is shalom. *Shalom* means peace, prosperity, health, and favor. Prophecy releases the favor and encouragement we need to move forward.

85. The prophetic word encourages us to seek God.

> For thus saith the LORD unto the house of Israel, Seek ye me,
> and ye shall live.
> —AMOS 5:4

The prophetic word can stir us up to draw closer to God. God's
voice draws us to Him. Prophets encourage us to seek God.

86. The prophetic word challenges us to consider our ways.

> Now therefore thus saith the LORD of hosts; Consider your
> ways.
> —HAGGAI 1:5

Prophets can challenge us to consider our ways when they are
contrary to the will of God. Prophecy can bring conviction and
repentance.

87. The prophetic words shake the heavens, earth, and sea.

> For thus saith the LORD of hosts; Yet once, it is a little while,
> and I will shake the heavens, and the earth, and the sea, and
> the dry land.
> —HAGGAI 2:6

The prophetic word can shake kingdoms and nations. The
heavens, earth, and sea were always prophetic terms representing
kingdoms and peoples.

88. The prophetic word challenges men to repent.

> Therefore say thou unto them, Thus saith the LORD of hosts;
> Turn ye unto me, saith the LORD of hosts, and I will turn unto
> you, saith the LORD of hosts.
> —ZECHARIAH 1:3

The prophetic word brings conviction and challenges men to turn away from things that are destructive. Repentance can save your life.

89. The prophetic word releases strength.

> Thus saith the LORD of hosts; Let your hands be strong, ye that hear in these days these words by the mouth of the prophets, which were in the day that the foundation of the house of the LORD of hosts was laid, that the temple might be built.
>
> —ZECHARIAH 8:9

We need the strength of the Lord. We cannot do the will of God in our own strength. Prophecy can strengthen our spirits.

90. The prophetic word is a word in season.

> The Lord GOD hath given me the tongue of the learned, that I should know how to speak a word in season to him that is weary: he wakeneth morning by morning, he wakeneth mine ear to hear as the learned.
>
> —ISAIAH 50:4

The word of the Lord is released at a *kairos* time. This means it is a word delivered in the perfect timing of the Lord at a right time in someone's life for breakthrough and progress.

91. The right word carries power.

> How forcible are right words!
>
> —JOB 6:25

The right word at the right time carries tremendous power and force. Power and force are needed for breakthrough.

92. The prophetic word is sweet to the taste.

How sweet are thy words unto my taste! yea, sweeter than honey to my mouth!

—PSALM 119:103

We should enjoy the word of the Lord as something pleasant to the taste.

93. The prophetic word gives light and understanding to the simple.

The entrance of thy words giveth light; it giveth understanding unto the simple.

—PSALM 119:130

Light is needed to move forward. Understanding is needed to make the right decisions. Those who lack light and understanding can receive it through the prophetic word. God does not desire us to be ignorant.

94. The prophetic word releases wisdom.

Get wisdom, get understanding: forget it not; neither decline from the words of my mouth.

—PROVERBS 4:5

Wisdom is needed to avoid bad decisions. Your decisions affect your life and destiny.

95. The prophetic word can release health to the bones.

Pleasant words are as an honeycomb, sweet to the soul, and health to the bones.

—PROVERBS 16:24

Healthy bones are essential to good health. Pleasant words release health to the bones.

96. The prophetic word guarantees that we have God's words in our mouth.

> And I have put my words in thy mouth, and I have covered thee in the shadow of mine hand, that I may plant the heavens, and lay the foundations of the earth, and say unto Zion, Thou art my people.
>
> —ISAIAH 51:16

Prophecy is God putting His words in our mouth. We simply speak the word placed in our mouth by God. The heavens were planted and the foundations of the earth laid through the word of the Lord.

97. The prophetic guarantees that our seed will have God's word in their mouths.

> As for me, this is my covenant with them, saith the LORD; My spirit that is upon thee, and my words which I have put in thy mouth, shall not depart out of thy mouth, nor out of the mouth of thy seed, nor out of the mouth of thy seed's seed, saith the LORD, from henceforth and for ever.
>
> —ISAIAH 59:21

God desires His word to go from generation to generation. Our children should also prophesy. Each generation can experience the blessing of prophecy.

98. The prophetic word causes joy and rejoicing.

> Thy words were found, and I did eat them; and thy word was unto me the joy and rejoicing of mine heart: for I am called by thy name, O LORD God of hosts.
>
> —JEREMIAH 15:16

Prophecy releases great joy to the recipient. The joy of the Lord is our strength. Jeremiah found the word, and it brought great joy to his life. We should rejoice in receiving and speaking the word of the Lord.

99. God causes us to hear His word through the prophetic.

> Arise, and go down to the potter's house, and there I will cause thee to hear my words.
>
> —JEREMIAH 18:2

You can hear the voice of the Lord. You can hear God's word in your spirit.

100. God's words release spirit and life.

> It is the spirit that quickeneth; the flesh profiteth nothing: the words that I speak unto you, they are spirit, and they are life.
>
> —JOHN 6:63

Prophecy is a spiritual container releasing the life of God. Because the word is spirit, it affects our spirits and the spirit realm.

Conclusion

*Where there is no prophecy the people cast off
restraint, but blessed is he who keeps the law.*

—PROVERBS 29:18, RSV

ROPHECY PROVIDES REVELATION to the purposes of God. It
is the revealed will of God for your life. "Where there is no
prophecy the people cast of restraint." "Casting off restraint"
is letting go of your goals and focus in life. You become passionless,
living an undisciplined, mediocre life. Without prophetic revelation we lose a grip on life and become like a wild person. Without
prophecy we become like a savage, never grasping the potential
God has placed within us. Prophecy can inspire within us a sense
of purpose that brings focus, determination, and discipline into our
lives.

The prophetic word will align our lives with the law, which is
the decree of God. Without prophetic vision we will be untrained
in the ways of God, living our lives without the discipline of God.
We are called to be disciples of Christ. A disciple is a disciplined
learner. The prophetic ministry will equip you with the advantage
of living under the discipline of God.

The disadvantage of not having prophecy released in your life is
that you will live your life in a vacuum. One translation of Proverbs
29:18 states that "without prophetic vision the people run wild"
(GW). In other words, they will live life taking risks with no control,
direction, uncultivated, out of rhythm, and out of reason.

The prophetic word brings order and structure to your life. God wants your life to mean something—your money, your efforts. The prophetic word of God causes you to live your life for something greater than yourself.

Life and time are speeding along so fast for all of us. We should be able to look back over our lives to say that we have accomplished the purpose God created us for. We should want to be able to confidently say, "I was here."

The prophetic word will allow you to live for eternal purpose and not temporal. It changes your value system. Once the revealed purpose of the Lord is known, you set your affections on things above, transcending this temporal world.

There are people who live their lives never knowing and obeying the prophetic purpose of God. The graveyard is one of the richest places in the earth. People live and die on the earth with so much potential for greatness. They never impact the world around them. Don't let your gravestone epitaph read: "It was like they were never here." "They settled for too little." "They never discovered the riches and treasures that were inside of them." "They lived for the temporal fading purposes, never living out God's eternal purposes."

Life before Christ can be so devastating and confusing. It's like having the wind knocked out of you. The prophetic word provides spiritual oxygen for life and destiny. Prophecy is the breath of life being released back into you. When God breathed into Adam, He released life and prophetic purpose into him.

We must understand that God will always give us pictures, maps, and directions to show us how we should be living our lives. His will for our lives is knowable. This is revealed by prophecy. Everything in the earth is trying to take us away from the original purposes of God for our lives. It dangles every kind of glitter in front of us. Its ultimate goal is to lead us down paths of destruction.

God, in His love and mercy, sends prophets and prophetic people with insight and direction. We must then make a decision to follow and align our lives with the revealed prophetic word. We must go to the cross. I am not talking about suffering. But where your desires are in conflict with God's desires, you must be willing to put those desires to death on the cross.

The moment you choose to align your life with the prophetic purpose of God, the Lord is watching and sends every resource you need to accomplish His prophetic purpose in your life. You're not in this world by chance. Embrace the prophetic anointing that gives you an advantage to live a rich and full life.

Notes

Chapter 1
Releasing the Lion's Roar

1. Blue Letter Bible, "All Dictionary Results for *'Reformation'*," http://www.blueletterbible.org/Search/Dictionary/viewTopic.cfm? type=getTopic&topic=Reformation (accessed July 30, 2012).

2. Blue Letter Bible, "Dictionary and Word Search for *parrēsia* (Strong's 3954)," http://www.blueletterbible.org/lang/lexicon/lexicon .cfm?strongs=G3954 (accessed July 30, 2012).

Chapter 2
The Prophetic Advantage

1. Net Bible, s.v. "*logion*," http://classic.net.bible.org/strong .php?id=3051 (accessed July 30, 2012).

2. Concordances.org, *Strong's Exhaustive Concordance*, s.v. "wisdom," http://concordances.org/hebrew/2451.htm (accessed July 31, 2012).

3. Charlene Israel, "George Washington Carver: Master Inventor, Artist," CBN News, http://www.cbn.com/cbnnews/us/2010/February/ George-Washington-Carver-Master-Inventor-Artist/ (accessed July 31, 2012).

4. Blue Letter Bible, "Dictionary and Word Search for *cowd* (Strong's 5475)," http://www.blueletterbible.org/lang/lexicon/lexicon. cfm?Strongs=H5475&t=KJV (accessed August 23, 2012).

5. *Webster's Revised Unabridged Dictionary Version* (Springfield, MA: C. & G. Merriam Co., 1913), s.v. "revelation."

Chapter 3
Prophets Are Builder

1. Blue Letter Bible, "Dictionary and Word Search for *synoikodomeō* (Strong's 4925)," http://www.blueletterbible.org/lang/lexicon/lexicon .cfm?Strongs=G4925&t=KJV (accessed July 31, 2012).

2. Blue Letter Bible, "Dictionary and Word Search for *epistērizō* (Strong's 1991)," http://www.blueletterbible.org/lang/lexicon/lexicon .cfm?strongs=G1991 (accessed August 1, 2012).

3. Blue Letter Bible, "Dictionary and Word Search for *blepō* (Strong's 991)," http://www.blueletterbible.org/lang/lexicon/lexicon .cfm?Strongs=G991&t=KJV (accessed August 17, 2012).

4. *Oxford Dictionaries Online*, s.v. "investigate," http:// oxforddictionaries.com/definition/english/investigate (accessed August 17, 2012).

Chapter 4
The Creative Force of Prophesy

1. Blue Letter Bible, "Dictionary and Word Search for *bara'* (Strong's 1254)," http://www.blueletterbible.org/lang/lexicon/lexicon .cfm?Strongs=H1254&t=KJV (accessed August 2, 2012).

2. *New Spirit-Filled Life Bible* (Nashville, TN: Thomas Nelson, 2002), 3, s.v. *"bara'."*

Chapter 5
Character in the Prophetic Ministry

1. Blue Letter Bible, "Dictionary and Word Search for *kardia* (Strong's 2588)," http://www.blueletterbible.org/lang/lexicon/lexicon .cfm?strongs=G2588 (accessed August 2, 2012).

2. Blue Letter Bible, "Dictionary and Word Search for *eilikrinēs* (Strong's 1506)," http://www.blueletterbible.org/lang/lexicon/lexicon .cfm?Strongs=G1506&t=KJV (accessed August 2, 2012.

3. Blue Letter Bible, "Dictionary and Word Search for *Pěnuw'el* (Strong's 6439)"," http://www.blueletterbible.org/lang/lexicon/lexicon .cfm?strongs=H6439 (accessed August 2, 2012.

4. Chabad.org, "Hayom Yom: Cheshvan 13," http://www.chabad .org/library/article_cdo/aid/5973/jewish/Hayom-Yom-Cheshvan-13 .htm (accessed August 6, 2012).

5. *Merriam-Webster Online Dictionary*, s.v. "conviction," http:// www.merriam-webster.com/dictionary/conviction (accessed August 3, 2012).

Chapter 6
Roadblocks to Accuracy

1. Blue Letter Bible, "Dictionary and Word Search for *mowqesh* (Strong's 4170)," http://www.blueletterbible.org/lang/lexicon/lexicon .cfm?Strongs=H4170&t=KJV (accessed August 17, 2012).
2. Orthodox Wiki, s.v. "repentance," http://en.orthodoxwiki.org/ Repentance (accessed August 7, 2012).

Chapter 7
The Voice of the Lord

1. *New Spirit-Filled Life Bible*, s.v. "Ps. 29:6."
2. Blue Letter Bible, "Dictionary and Word Search for *nadiyb* (Strong's 5081)," http://www.blueletterbible.org/lang/lexicon/lexicon .cfm?Strongs=H5081&t=KJV (accessed August 3, 2012).

Chapter 8
Prophetic Diversity

1. Blue Letter Bible, "Dictionary and Word Search for *metadidōmi* (Strong's 3330)," http://www.blueletterbible.org/lang/lexicon/lexicon .cfm?strongs=G3330 (accessed August 3, 2012).

Chapter 10
Seek to Excel in Prophecy

1. Blue Letter Bible, "Dictionary and Word Search for *zēlōtēs* (Strong's 2208)," http://www.blueletterbible.org/lang/lexicon/lexicon .cfm?strongs=G2208 (accessed August 7, 2012).
2. Blue Letter Bible, "Dictionary and Word Search for *hexis* (Strong's 1838)," http://www.blueletterbible.org/lang/lexicon/lexicon .cfm?strongs=G1838 (accessed August 7, 2012).
3. BibleStudyTools.com, s.v. "*martureo*," http://www .biblestudytools.com/lexicons/greek/kjv/martureo.html (accessed August 8, 2012).
4. Blue Letter Bible, "Dictionary and Word Search for *apokalyptō* (Strong's 601)," http://www.blueletterbible.org/lang/lexicon/lexicon .cfm?Strongs=G601&t=KJV (accessed August 8, 2012).

5. Blue Letter Bible, "Dictionary and Word Search for *shama'* (Strong's 8085)," http://www.blueletterbible.org/lang/lexicon/lexicon.cfm?strongs=H8085 (accessed August 8, 2012).

6. Blue Letter Bible, "Dictionary and Word Search for *batsar* (Strong's 1219)," http://www.blueletterbible.org/lang/lexicon/lexicon.cfm?Strongs=H1219&t=KJV (accessed August 22, 2012).

Chapter 12
Angels and the Prophetic Word

1. Blue Letter Bible, "Dictionary and Word Search for *Machanayim* (Strong's 4266)," http://www.blueletterbible.org/lang/lexicon/lexicon.cfm?Strongs=H4266&t=KJV (accessed August 5, 2012).

2. Blue Letter Bible, "Dictionary and Word Search for *nataph* (Strong's 5197)," http://www.blueletterbible.org/lang/lexicon/lexico.cfm?Strongs=H5197&t=KJV (accessed August 5, 2012).

3. Blue Letter Bible, "Dictionary and Word Search for *marmar* (Strong's 4843)," http://www.blueletterbible.org/lang/lexicon/lexicon.cfm?strongs=H4843 (accessed August 6, 2012).

Chapter 13
The Plumb Line

1. Blue Letter Bible, "Dictionary and Word Search for *mishmereth* (Strong's 4931)," http://www.blueletterbible.org/lang/lexicon/lexicon.cfm?strongs=H8104 (accessed August 6, 2012).

2. Blue Letter Bible, "Dictionary and Word Search for *shamar* (Strong's 8104)," http://www.blueletterbible.org/lang/lexicon/lexicon.cfm?strongs=H4931 (accessed August 6, 2012).

3. Blue Letter Bible, "Dictionary and Word Search for *massa'* (Strong's 4853)," http://www.blueletterbible.org/lang/lexicon/lexicon.cfm?strongs=H4853 (accessed August 6, 2012).

4. Blue Letter Bible, "Dictionary and Word Search for *kairos* (Strong's 2540)," http://www.blueletterbible.org/lang/lexicon/lexicon.cfm?strongs=G2540 (accessed August 5, 2012).

5. Ernest B. Gentile, *Your Sons and Daughters Shall Prophesy* (Grand Rapids, MI: Chosen Books, 1999), 46.

6. Ibid.

7. Ibid.

8. *Spirit-Filled Life Bible* (Nashville, TN: Thomas Nelson, 1991), 1183.

9. Blue Letter Bible, "Dictionary and Word Search for *naba'* (Strong's 5012)," http://www.blueletterbible.org/lang/lexicon/lexicon .cfm?strongs=H5012 (accessed August 20, 2012).

10. *Spirit-Filled Life Bible*, 407.

11. Ibid., 648.

12. Ibid., 1170.

13. Ibid., 1092.

14. Gentile, *Your Sons and Daughters Shall Prophesy*, 46.

15. Ibid.

16. Ibid.

17. Ibid.

18. Ibid.

Chapter 14
The Spirit and Power of Elijah

1. Bound4Life, "Statistics," http://bound4life.com/statistics/ (accessed August 6, 2012).

2. Francis Frangipane, *The Three Battlegrounds* (Cedar Rapids, IA: Arrow Publications, Inc., 2006), 132.